WORDS
OF
LIFE

WORDS OF LIFE

**EASTER EDITION
JANUARY–APRIL 1989**

HODDER AND STOUGHTON
and
THE SALVATION ARMY

ABBREVIATIONS USED FOR
BIBLE VERSIONS

AV   Authorised (King James) Version
GNB   Good News Bible
JB   Jerusalem Bible
JBP   J. B. Phillips – The New Testament in Modern English, 1972 edition
LB   The Living Bible – Kenneth Taylor
JM   James Moffatt
NEB   The New English Bible
NIV   New International Version
RSV   Revised Standard Version
WB   William Barclay – The New Testament

Permission to quote from The New English Bible, Second Edition © 1970, has been granted by the Oxford and Cambridge University Presses; from The Good News Bible by the British and Foreign Bible Society and Wm. Collins Sons and Co. Ltd; from The New Testament in Modern English (J. B. Phillips) © 1972, from the New International Version; and from the Revised Standard Version Bible © 1946, 1952, 1971 by the Division of Education and Ministry, National Council of the Churches of Christ in the USA.

British Library Cataloguing in Publication Data

Words of life. Jan.–Apr. 1989–
  1. Christian life – Daily readings
  242'.2

  ISBN 0-340-48887-5

CONTENTS

'Unity amid diversity'

RICHES OF PRAISE IN SONG

The book of Psalms is the hymn book of the Old Testament. There are many other Old Testament poetic passages which could fit into *Psalms* quite happily, but this collection of 150 separate poems is unique. The poems are divided into five books. It has been suggested that this division mirrors the division of the Pentateuch, the books of Moses, the first five books of the Old Testament.

Book 1.	Psalms	1– 41	Parallels Genesis	accent on Man
Book 2.	Psalms	42– 72	Parallels Exodus	accent on Israel
Book 3.	Psalms	73– 89	Parallels Leviticus	accent on Sanctity
Book 4.	Psalms	90–106	Parallels Numbers	accent on All Men
Book 5.	Psalms	107–150	Parallels Deuteronomy	accent on Obedience

Such parallels are by no means exact, but they do provide a useful focus of attention.

At intervals this year we shall study selected psalms. The first ten days of the new year will be spent on Psalms 1–10. During mid lent we shall look at the Songs of Ascents, Psalms 120–134, and other psalms in the succeeding volumes.

A PSALM OF CONTRASTS

READING PSALM 1
'Blessed is the man who walks not in the counsel of the wicked,
**   nor stands in the way of sinners, nor sits in the seat of scoffers;**
But his delight is in the law of the Lord,
**   And on his law he meditates day and night' (vv. 1,2, RSV).**

Good – bad. Wise – foolish. Fruitful – withered. Standing fast – blown away. Psalm 1 is a psalm of contrasts, showing the powerful effect of Hebrew poetry, where *ideas* in contrast or in parallel are used to build the structure of a poem. Rhythm and rhyme of words are not so important. The rhythm of *ideas* is paramount. So Psalms are ideal poetry for translation. Rhythm and rhyme are usually lost when turned into a different language. *Ideas* remain. *(A Wisdom Psalm. Other examples – Psalms 37, 73, 112 etc.)*

This simple psalm has a complex structure. The blessed (v. 1) balance the wicked (v. 4). Delight in the law parallels meditation on the law (v. 2) and so on. The Law, Prophets, and Writings (Wisdom literature) form the three sections of Old Testament Scripture. Two are mentioned in this psalm. Lack of wisdom (v. 1) is contrasted to delight in the law (v. 2). It is almost like a puzzle, spotting most comparisons and contrasts in these six simple verses.

Psalm 1 is spiritual. It is not about material things. The Psalmist is aware, as we are, that wickedness sometimes brings prosperity in this life. He contrasts the *blessing* (v. 1) of the spiritual with the *perishing* (v. 6) of the wicked. There is no middle way. Jesus offers the same choice: a narrow road to life or broad road to destruction. We must be tolerant of others. We must be flexible in what we expect from them. But the choice is plain, commitment to the wisdom of righteousness, or surrender to the foolishness of evil.

PRAYER SUBJECT: *Praising God for poetry, especially the Psalms.*

PRAYER: *We praise you, Lord, for the clever, technical poetry of the Psalms, which is a delight to scholars and lovers of poetry. Help us, Lord, to discover in these poems the great spiritual truths they contain.*

TRUTH RE-APPLIED

READING PSALM 2

'He said to me, "You are my son, today I have begotten you.
   Ask of me, and I will make the nations your heritage,
      and the ends of the earth your possession.
You shall break them with a rod of iron,
   And dash them in pieces like a potter's vessel"' (vv. 7b–9, RSV).

Acts 4:25,26;
Matt. 3:17;
Acts 13:33;
Heb. 1:5; 5:5;
2 Pet. 1:17

A Royal
Psalm: Other
examples
Pss.
18,20,21,45,
72,101,110,
132,144

John 10:13

Today's psalm is quoted often in the New Testament. Though originally a coronation psalm, sung in praise of newly crowned kings of David's lineage, we can see why it was re-applied to Jesus. No earthly king could ever hope to 'make the ends of the earth his possession' (v. 8). Only God in Jesus can do that.

Both Jewish and Christian commentators see a description of the Messiah in Psalm 2. Two of his titles, 'The Lord's anointed' (v. 2) and 'Son of God' (v. 7) derive from this Psalm. The king, in ancient times, was regarded as 'Son of God,' i.e. God's representative on earth. He was more than an ambassador. An ambassador is simply a 'hired man'. The king was a son, one who should have the whole interests of God at heart. How sadly practice fell short of theory! King after evil king succeeded to the throne both in Israel and Judah.

Jesus alone fulfilled the requirements of a Son, and he alone remains worthy of the title.

But v. 9? Surely that can't apply to Jesus? 'Breaking' the nations with a rod of iron appears in some translations – and in all New Testament references to Psalm 2 – as 'rule'. But that hardly solves the problem. We see New Testament truth in the psalm, but must never forget its original setting, a setting where 'eye for eye' and 'tooth for tooth' was the regulation. Something of that still exists in each of us.

TO THINK
ABOUT

Do the desires for revenge and domination so freely expressed in the Psalms teach me something about my own inner motivations?

READING PSALM 3
'I have so many enemies, Lord,
So many who turn against me!
They talk about me and say,
"God will not help him"' (v. 1, GNB).

Psalm 3 is the first one headed 'A Psalm of David.' Apart from 10 and 33 the rest of Book I are all 'Psalms of David'. At first such a heading only meant the psalm was used in David's court – or that of his successors. Later it was taken to mean David himself composed it. But this heading has an addition – 'After he ran away from his son Absalom'. How personal that makes it. We can see David, in terror of his life, hiding from one whom he loves. His only hope is in the Lord himself.

2 Sam. 15:14

The instruction *Selah* occurs three times in this psalm. No one is quite sure what it means. Various explanations are that it indicates

(a) The congregation were supposed to shout a response.
(b) The signal for a musical interlude. Singing a chorus?
(c) The worshippers should bow to the ground.
(d) Simply a point at which to pause.

see Ps. 9

These ideas have one thing in common. Selah is there to help the psalm to be used in congregational worship. How strange! Such a personal psalm has three sets of instructions for the congregation to take part. But that is a feature of this remarkable book. The most personal songs are the favourites for use in worship. When we speak from the heart, when we are honest with ourselves our words have meaning for a wider congregation.

Praise God that the psalmists, from David onwards, have shared their innermost feelings. Praise him, too, that we can express those feelings in their words in our congregational worship.

FOR PRAISE

SO MUCH IN SO SMALL A SPACE

READING PSALM 4
'Many . . . pray: "Give us more blessings, O Lord.
Look on us with kindness!"
But the joy that you have given me is more than they will ever have
with all their corn and wine' (vv. 6,7, GNB).

Every verse of Psalm 4 could be the subject of a long article. E.g. *RSV* translates the first verse, 'Thou hast given me room when I was in distress.' What a lovely thought! How the distressed soul needs space! How often we hear the cry from the young, and not-so-young 'Don't fence me in!' Our psalmist knows God sees our distress and gives us room.

Or again, so soon after Christmas, on the eleventh day of the twelve-day feast, how comforting it is to read the psalmist's statement and to know that even though there was no room for God's Son, God still gives us room!

Verse two laments man's tendency not to tell the truth. Verse three reminds us the Lord has chosen us for his own – if we count ourselves among the righteous. What a large statement that is! Verse four (*RSV*) asks us to 'be angry and sin not.' Five asks us to 'Offer the right sacrifices to the Lord.'

Rom. 6:11

But verses six and seven contain today's seed thought. They take us back to Psalm 1 where we saw the psalmist's concern with spiritual matters.

Many, sadly, still today are more concerned with material things than spiritual. Their priorities are wrong. Even redistribution of wealth is a spiritual problem. Wars resulting in famine spring from spiritual malaise. Pollution, greed, exploitation all have a spiritual root – or rather owe their existence to lack of spiritual roots.

TO THINK
ABOUT

When the spiritual dimension is taken care of, the material will fall into place.

THE TERRIBLE TONGUE

READING PSALM 5

> 'Their throat is an open sepulchre
> They flatter with their tongue.
> Make them bear their guilt, O God . . .
> Cast them out, for they have rebelled against thee' (vv. 9,10, RSV).

C. S. Lewis notes his surprise, when he began to read the Psalms, at finding how much they had to say about evil speaking. He says 'I had half expected that in a simpler and more violent age (!) when more evil was done with the knife, the big stick, and the firebrand, less would be done by talk. But in reality the Psalmists mention hardly any kind of evil more often than this one, which the most civilised societies share' – and he then goes on to quote the first line of today's highlighted verse.

Psalm 5 also contains another very common feature of the Psalms, a prayer for the destruction or rejection of the psalmist's enemies. This always seems to be on the basis that the other man is wicked, while I am righteous. It is a danger we all face – to consider that because someone opposes us they are not only wrong, but wicked. Often, it may be true – for how many of us are completely righteous? But because it is often true that does not mean we can assume it is always true. We shall return to this important factor in the Psalms on a number of occasions. For the moment we do well to pray about it.

Help me, O Lord, to discern the difference between different opinions and evil intentions. May I never confuse one with the other. A PRAYER

A PENITENTIAL PSALM

READING PSALM 6
   'Turn, O Lord, save my life;
deliver me for the sake of thy steadfast love.
For in death there is no remembrance of thee;
   in Sheol who can give thee praise?' (v. 4,5, RSV).

Although the setting of this psalm is still one where the psalmist sees himself plagued by enemies, it breathes a different atmosphere from Psalm 5. We sense the writer identifies himself with the evil-doers from whom he seeks to be freed. He is enslaved by his circumstances. Every night he sheds floods of tears. He longs for freedom from the evil which surrounds him.

In our modern world we hear similar cries. I want to be free – but how? The writer seems to be experiencing the same pressures an addict faces. He knows how evil his surroundings are; he sees the harm his enemies/friends are doing him, yet those are the only surroundings he has. Take them away, remove the evil, and you also remove the little that is good. How many people stay in an environment which drags them down because that is the only one where they find any comfort and support at all. In a new environment they may become completely confused, bewildered and desperate.

Take the evil away and what is left? For the writer of Psalm 6, very little. His hope is only for this life. He has no hope for the next. He sees himself being cut off completely from God. Yet still he prays to be released from the evil which surrounds him.

The hope that we hold out to a lost world, the world of the abandoned and the oppressed, of the addict and the alcoholic, is a different hope, an eternal hope.

FOR
THOUGHT
The Psalmist was afraid death would cut him off from God. We know different. We know that hope is not just for this life, but also for a life beyond the grave.

SORROW OR SELF-RIGHTEOUSNESS?

READING PSALM 7
'O Lord my God, if I have done this, if there is wrong in my hands,
If I have requited my friend with evil
or plundered my enemy without cause,
Let the enemy pursue me and overtake me' (vv. 3,4,5a, RSV).

Here is a good example of how different things can appear when looked at from a different angle. Looked at one way, we could imagine the writer of Psalm 7 is saying with over-bearing pride, he is sure his own actions are absolutely good – 'If I have *ever* done anything like that, then "lay my soul in the dust."' We sense he feels he's never done a thing wrong in his life – and has been remarkably charitable towards his dreadful opponents, his 'enemies'!

But from the traditional heading of Psalm 7 we can get a quite different angle. The heading says 'A Psalm of David concerning Cush a Benjamite'. Was Cush a friend or an enemy? We can't tell. But if he was a friend, then v. 3 takes on quite a new character. Here we have David half afraid that one of his wrong actions might be to blame for his friend's fate. Verses 4 & 5 also take on quite a different flavour. They become a song of penitence, as in Psalm 6, rather than a proud statement of self-righteousness, as in Psalm 5. How we would love to know more!

Forgive the sins I have confessed to thee   A PRAYER
Forgive the secret sins I do not see.
O guide me, love me, and my keeper be,
Dear Lord, Amen.

(C. M. Battersby)

A PSALM OF POWER

READING PSALM 8
'What is man that thou art mindful of him.
And the son of man that thou dost care for him?
. . . Thou hast given him dominion over the works of thy hands'
(vv. 4,6, RSV).

We each have power, limited but nonetheless real. A baby has power over its mother. The baby cries – mum responds. Baby soon learns to use that power to get its own way. Only very sure and confident parents can resist baby-power and take care of baby's needs at the same time. But some over-grown babies have enormous power. Some control vast factories; some have union empires; some have hordes of armed men under their control; some, indeed, may have access to buttons that could wipe the human race from the earth.

In the face of such power it is tempting for ordinary people to feel insignificant. It is just as tempting for others to feel over-important.

The power of this psalm is reflected by its use elsewhere in Scripture. We often look for Old Testament quotations in the New, but Psalm 8 is actually parodied in the Old Testament itself *(See also Job 7:17f)*. Imitation is the sincerest form of flattery. Parody runs it a close second. Job complains God pays him too much attention, while the Psalmist is surprised that the great God has time for him. Either way Psalm 8 expresses what we all feel intensely. The greatness of God in contrast to our own smallness. At the same time it assures us we are important to God.

You humbly came to save me
    Of that I am aware.
But is it ever really true,
    That I can be of use to you?

Your glory fills the heavens
    My smallness makes me fear.
Yet God in Christ assures me still,
    There is a space for me to fill.

PRAYER SUBJECT: *For a right relationship with God.*

PRAYER: *We confess, Lord, that sometimes the sense of your power overwhelms us. At other times our own self-centredness gets the better of us. Help us to get the balance right, through our Lord and Saviour, Jesus Christ.*

GOD FORGETS?

READING PSALM 9 (especially vv. 1,2,15–20)
'The needy shall not always be forgotten,
and the hope of the poor shall not perish for ever' (v. 18, RSV).

The psalmists are often preoccupied by the idea that justice is a long time coming. Over and again they complain that the wicked prosper and the righteous suffer. They look forward to a day when God will judge, and the wicked get what they deserve. But that judgment is delayed. It does not come as soon as we would hope and expect.

Why does it not come? God, says the Psalmist, 'forgets'. 'The idea of forgetting is one of the figures of speech adopted by the psalmist in order to express the "delayed action" of God' (Norman Snaith).

This delayed action also appears in Psalm 10, which Leonard Griffith entitles 'God Hides.' Such expressions remind us of the many situations where God appears to be absent. Often we think he is absent when we're in trouble. It is then that so many of us call on him and complain. But when things go well materially there are just as many for whom God appears to be absent. Exceptions occur, of course, and the USA with its high proportion of church-goers may be one. Or is it such an exception? Is God really present amongst those who call on his name in prosperity? Or is he simply delaying judgment?

We have the Pharisees in the New Testament, and also many prosperous, self-satisfied people in the Old to cite as examples. It may appear that God 'remembers' those who prosper and who worship him loudly, but take heed of the psalmist's words

'The needy shall not always be forgotten,
and the hope of the poor shall not perish for ever'

It is not always those who make most noise about their A THOUGHT
belief in God who are closest to him.

GOD HIDES?

READING PSALM 10
'Why dost thou stand afar off, O Lord? Why dost thou hide thyself in times of trouble? . . . In the pride of his countenance the wicked does not seek him; all his thoughts are, "There is no God" (vv. 1,4b, RSV).

Yesterday we asked 'Why is judgment delayed?' Today we ask 'Why does God hide?' and in so doing we shall, hopefully, come closer to an answer to both questions. The following ideas are from Leonard Griffith.

God hides so that we may rediscover him as he actually is
If God were always obvious, even to eyes which are clouded by unbelief and sin, he would not be God at all but an idol of our own devising. Jesus taught us to address God familiarly as 'Our Father' – but added 'Who art in Heaven.'

Matt. 6:9
Exod. 20:4

God hides so that we shall look for him where he is actually to be found
Some think mistakenly of God as if he was an external factor we could control and bring to bear from the outside on our troubles if we prayed hard enough, but the Bible teaches that God is an internal factor always at work within our human affairs. Many of our troubles are the result of our refusal to recognise him and work along with his purpose.

Acts 17:28

God hides so that we might be driven to an exercise of true faith
What need would there be for faith if God were always visible?

Heb. 11:1

God hides so that we may rise to a higher level of spiritual perception
What need is there to strive after higher things if God is always visible?

TODAY'S
THOUGHT

'Blessed are the pure in heart, for they shall see God'.
(Matthew 5:8)

A FRAGMENTED CHURCH
(Acts 18 and 1 Corinthians)

The ministry of Jesus was limited in time and place – just a few months in rural Galilee, plus a whirlwind impact on the city of Jerusalem. However, Paul's ministry in Corinth demonstrates how Jesus' gospel is as relevant in large colourful centres of population, as in rural Galilee. May we also find in our study that it is as relevant today as it was then.

Our study starts with the founding of the Corinthian church, recorded in Acts 18. We then go on to discover the riches of Paul's thinking in the advice which he conveys to the infant church from his next extended stay in the great city of Ephesus.

Study passages will not always be continuous. Related ideas are often found a few verses apart. Imagine you are a member of this divided church in Corinth. You would naturally want to read the whole letter at once to get an answer to the church's problems. Try to make time for this at some point during the more detailed study. For quick reading *The Living Bible* or *J. B. Phillips* are probably best. In study we shall often refer to *RSV* or *NIV*.

ATHENS TO CORINTH

READING ACTS 18:1–6
'After this he left Athens and went to Corinth . . . He argued in the synagogue every sabbath, and persuaded Jews and Greeks' (vv. 1,4, RSV).

Acts
16,11–17:15

Acts
17:16–34

Acts 18:2

Athens to Corinth was about 75 miles. Paul would go by boat to Cenchreae, then overland a few miles to Corinth, a vast town of half a million people. After a successful ministry in Macedonia, Paul on his own had limited success in Athens. He probably dreaded what might happen in Corinth. Imagine his relief at finding Aquila and Priscilla. They had been thrown out of Rome by Claudius' edict against Jews in AD 49. They would know the difficulties of settling into a new environment.

Their support was welcome, but Paul eagerly waited for Silas and Timothy to arrive from Macedonia. Alone, he had preached a gospel for intellectuals in Athens. His arguments were good. He made an impression. But his preaching lacked its usual force. He still argued in the synagogues in Corinth, but again with very little success. Three factors changed the situation.

v. 5
v. 6
1 Cor. 2:2

1. The arrival of Silas and Timothy
2. Turning to the Gentiles
3. Paul's determination to preach only Christ crucified

When we blame our circumstances for lack of success, it's usually just an excuse. But Paul's experience shows this is not always so. There was some failure on his part, certainly. But he was able to fully realise and express God's task for him only when circumstances changed. When Silas and Timothy came; when he made the right decision to include the whole community, AND to preach Christ alone – only then was Paul able to fulfil his complete ministry.

TO PONDER

*To become more effective do **I** need to change, must my **circumstances** change, or must I start concentrating on **Christ alone**?*

CHRISTIANS AND JEWS

READING ACTS 18:7–17
'When Gallio was proconsul of Achaia, the Jews made a united attack upon Paul and brought him before the tribunal' (v. 12, RSV).

A firm date for Biblical events is often impossible to give. Luke's account of Paul's activity in Acts leaves many gaps, but we can use a few specific pieces of information to gain a good understanding of Paul's movements. Mention of Gallio is the most specific of all. An inscription found at Delphi enables Gallio's year of consulship to be dated AD 51–52. We therefore know Paul founded the church in Corinth some time in AD 51.

Today's passage also shows how the opposition to Paul used the resources of the Roman empire – and also something of the way Rome handled their complaints. Jews had a fair degree of self-determination. Civil disputes were largely left to the synagogues to settle. If a Jew had a complaint against another Jew he would not dream of going to the Roman authorities, but would abide by the synagogue ruling. The Roman authorities were happy with this as it saved them a great deal of trouble.

Gallio was so accustomed to letting Jews pass their own judgements, he did not bat an eyelid when Sosthenes was beaten by the Jewish authorities. We can understand the Jews' difficulty. Most saw Christianity as a threat to their existence, rather than a fulfilment of everything in the Old Testament. Today's Christians should remember this, and treat Jews with sensitivity.

Many Jews see the holocaust perpetrated by Hitler as a natural outcome of Christian antagonism to the Jews. A THOUGHT

Father in Heaven, we pray for greater understanding between Christians and Jews. Help us, so that neither blames the other for past difficulties and atrocities. Help us, through greater, charitable understanding to ensure that such atrocities do not and cannot occur in the future. A PRAYER

A PRODIGIOUS OUTPUT

READING ACTS 18:18–22 (19:1,8,10; 20:1–3)
'Paul sailed for Syria (18), Ephesus (19), Caesarea, the (Jerusalem) church, Antioch (22) Ephesus (19:1) Macedonia (20:1) Greece (20:2)'

Paul's Journeys and the Letters to Corinth. Today's reading is a geography lesson, which may help us to understand Paul's correspondence with Corinth.

1. Corinthian church founded AD 51. Stayed 'many days.'
2. Boat to Ephesus. Left Aquila and Priscilla there. Paul did not stay.
3. Boat to Caesarea.
4. Short visit to 'the church' (in Jerusalem?).
5. Via Antioch, overland to Ephesus. Stayed over two years.
6. Via Macedonia, to Greece, probably Corinth, for three months.

Paul tells us he wrote at least four letters to Corinth:

1 Cor. 5:9

The first *before* 1 Corinthians. Paul says 'I wrote to you in my letter.'

The second, from Ephesus, is our 1 Corinthians.

see 2 Cor. 2:3–9

The third was a 'severe letter' following a 'painful visit'. This visit, probably made from Ephesus, is not recorded in Acts. Ephesus was only three days from Corinth by boat.

Acts 20:3

The fourth is our 2 Corinthians, made before the visit to Corinth recorded 'to finalise the collection for the Jerusalem church.

TO THINK ABOUT

Paul did so much more than is shown by the combined record of Acts and Paul's own New Testament letters. What we read is just a fragment of his vast activity, and his gigantic reservoir of thought.

ELOQUENT APOLLOS

READING ACTS 18:24–28

'Apollos . . . was an eloquent man, well versed in the scriptures. He had been instructed in the way of the Lord; and being fervent in spirit, he spoke and taught accurately the things concerning Jesus, though he knew only the baptism of John' (vv. 24,25, RSV).

Eloquent Apollos was a disciple of John the Baptist. John's disciples seem to have still been a separate and recognisable group. Not all his followers can have gone over to Jesus, and in a day when communications were difficult, small groups survived until long after the ministry, death and resurrection of Jesus. They would be men prepared for the coming of the Messiah, ready for the news of Jesus. But it was still a bold, courageous step for Priscilla and Aquila to take hold of Apollos and expound the Scriptures to him anew. Acts 19:3

In today's world many are searching with a partial understanding. They look for answers to their problems. They look for fulfilment of their expectations. We no longer meet disciples of John, but we meet members of other faiths, sincere and devout people, ready to talk with us. We meet young men and women with a partial knowledge of Christianity, a vague belief in God and some sense of right and wrong.

All too often such people find little to help them in the 'take-it-or-leave-it' atmosphere of some modern churches and Army corps. What they need is personal conversation, exposition of the scriptures from a position of knowledge and a breadth of vision which will see in them great potential for the Kingdom of God.

Do I know the Scriptures well enough to expound them to another who is seeking for answers? Am I prepared to make the effort to study so that I can expound the way of God more accurately? TO ASK MYSELF

Inspire me, Lord, through the study of your Word. Help me to share it with others. Increase my appetite for the riches of your wisdom. A PRAYER

WORKING TOGETHER

READING 1 CORINTHIANS 1:1–3 (Acts 18:1–17)
'Paul, called by the will of God to be an apostle of Christ Jesus, and our brother Sosthenes' (v. 1, RSV).

Sosthenes, the synagogue ruler from Corinth *(Acts 18:17)* was with Paul at Ephesus when this letter was written. Paul knew, more than anyone, how important it was to have help when spreading the gospel. On his own, Paul found it difficult to cope.

Usually Timothy helped Paul with letters *(2 Corinthians 1:1; Philippians 1:1; Colossians 1:1)*. Silas also helped with the letters to Thessalonika; Romans was dictated to Tertius, who was the 'writer' of the letter! *(Romans 16:22)*. What effect 'co-authors' or scribes had on the thought of Paul's letters is uncertain, but we can imagine Timothy and Silas helping a lot.

We know nothing about Sosthenes, apart from this verse and the Acts reference. It is hard to think of him influencing Paul's thinking, but Paul was more flexible than first impressions indicate. Some of his advice to the Corinthian church could well have come from Sosthenes, himself a Corinthian, who would know the city well.

Many matters dealt with in this letter arose from questions people in Corinth had asked *(see 1:11; 7:1)*. So Paul was dependent upon others even for the subject matter of his letter. It was born out of real crises, out of real conflicts, in a social not just an individual situation.

PRAYER SUBJECT: *Co-workers in the gospel.*
PRAYER: *We confess, Lord, it is sometimes hard to work with others in spreading the gospel. Our ideas are different. Relationships are sometimes strained. Forgive us for our limited vision. Enable us to learn from Paul's example, to take the advice of others, and always to use the help available from fellow Christians as we try to spread your word.*

POOR LITTLE RICH CHURCH

READING 1 CORINTHIANS 1:4–9, 26–31
'You do not lack any spiritual gift' (v. 7, NIV).
'No-one may boast before him' (v. 29, NIV).

Corinth was a mixed city. Different nationalities, races, religions, different degrees of poverty and wealth. All the flotsam and jetsam of a large, bustling port whose ships came from the four corners of the earth; hangers-on of overland trading caravans, going as far as India, and even perhaps China; rich, grasping businessmen; conceited scholars; priests of different religions; hordes of prostitutes; swarms of sailors; masses of ordinary workers. All converged on Corinth, a hive of activity, and den of iniquity surpassed only in scale by our large, modern cities.

Amongst this variety a small group of mainly poor people come to know Christ through the preaching of Paul, assisted by Silas and Timothy. Some are Jews, the majority probably gentiles. They receive the Spirit with enthusiasm. They enjoy every blessing he gives. Their new-found faith is expressed in exuberant freedom. They prophesy, testify, speak in tongues, heal, teach, and 'eagerly wait for our Lord Jesus Christ to be revealed'. In every way they are rich in the Spirit. But with riches comes danger.

v. 7

It is tempting to rely on riches. Spiritual gifts are so *wonderful that their enjoyment may supplant the supreme gift, hiding our complete dependence on Jesus* Christ and the salvation he offers. When we receive spiritual gifts, just as when we receive earthly riches, we may forget their source. So Paul reminds his poor church with the rich gifts, that none of us can boast in the presence of God.

There is nothing here provided by human industry, but QUOTATION
everything is provided by Divine Providence.
(St. Francis of Assisi)

FOUR FACTIONS

READING 1 CORINTHIANS 1:10–15
'It has been reported to me by Chloe's people that there is quarrelling among you, my brethren' (v. 11, RSV).

It is a mistake to consider church disunity a new phenomenon. Here (55 AD), at least four rival groups existed within the Corinthian church.

see 5:1–13 **1. 'I belong to Paul' (v. 12a)** LIBERTINES, probably a few among the first believers in Corinth. After hearing Paul talk of abolishing the law, they thought if they just believed the gospel they could do as they liked.

1:18–25 **2. 'I belong to Apollos' (v. 12b)** PHILOSOPHERS. Apollos was a learned Alexandrian Jew who knew Greek philosophy. This group probably thought themselves a little better intellectually than other Corinthian Christians.

Chs. 8 & 9 **3. 'I belong to Cephas' (v. 12c)** LEGALISTS probably a group who thought Christian life required strict adherence to Jewish Law.

10:1–13; 15:1–19 **4. 'I belong to Christ' (v. 12d)** MYSTICS. They probably thought themselves superior to the others, following Christ alone.

Each preserves an element of the truth.
  (1) We have *freedom* in Christ;
  (2) Depth of spiritual life can be helped through using our *intellect*;
  (3) The Jewish *law* is of value to Christians;
  (4) We can have *direct communion* with our Lord.

Together, each could learn from the other and profit from the other's emphasis on one aspect of the truth. None has the whole truth. As rivals they are a scandal and only serve to place a stumbling block in the path of seekers after truth.

QUOTATION *I would follow Christ – if it were not for the Christians.*
(Mahatma Gandhi)

PHILOSOPHERS BEWARE!

READING 1 CORINTHIANS 1:13–25
'Christ did not send me to baptise but, to preach the Good News, and not to preach that in the terms of philosophy in which the crucifixion of Christ cannot be expressed' (v. 17, JB).

Paul is not in the business of clever preaching. He knows his limitations, and admits them – as we shall see tomorrow. This does not stop him using his intellect, and agonising over all the intellectual problems of faith. His letters contain many intellectual, even philosophical arguments. But it is rare for anyone to become a Christian through intellectual conviction alone. _(2:3,4)_

Intellectual conviction is fine for those who have the brain power, but when it is laid down as a requirement for acceptance into the Christian faith it sets up a false barrier. It is like any other personal quality or ritual demand. Once it is made an absolute requirement it can become a hindrance rather than a help.

The same can even be said of baptism. Paul recognised the divisions it could cause. I'm sure he would recognise, too, that preaching can have the same effect. _(vv. 13–16)_ Those brought to a knowledge of Christ by a particular preacher can all too easily follow the preacher instead of Christ himself. For this reason Christians must always concentrate on the message, rather than the techniques of putting the message across. They must always concentrate on Christ, rather than on their own performance; concentrate on the source of wisdom, rather than on wisdom itself.

What helps do I really need in order to be able to concentrate on Christ supremely? TO PONDER

FEAR AND TREMBLING – AND THE POWER OF THE SPIRIT

READING 1 CORINTHIANS 2:1–10a

'Far from relying on any power of my own, I came among you in great "fear and trembling" and in my speeches and the sermons that I gave, there were none of the arguments that belong to philosophy; only a demonstration of the power of the Spirit' (vv. 3, 4, JB).

Rom. 8:22

1 Cor. 13:12

Paul often contrasts this world with the next. Here there is inward groaning. There, there is freedom and glory. But in Christ Jesus, through the power of the Spirit, we can gain a glimpse of what the next world will be. We see but 'a dim reflection' for our infinite, temporary, earthly bodies cannot take in the whole glory of God.

Acts 18:5

see Monday, par. 3

We may go in 'fear and trembling' before other people, – as anyone who has ever spoken in public, or had anything to do with public order will testify. We should, theoretically, be more fearful before God. If mere people can terrify us, how much worse to face God! Instead we find that God can empower us in the Spirit. This may not make a vast, visible difference. Paul remained nervous. He was heartily relieved when Silas and Timothy arrived to help. He still used 'none of the arguments that belong to philosophy' (v. 4). Perhaps he had learnt that lesson in Athens some weeks before! He did not even succumb to the Corinthian temptation of relying on the sensational spiritual gifts available. Instead he recognised his weakness and remained aware of God's strength.

It's not always possible to say 'It was good enough for Paul, so it's good enough for me,' or we would still be using quill pens. But this is an instance where we can say that. Weakness, backed up by the power of the Spirit was good enough for Paul. May God help us to realise it is good enough for us.

QUOTATION

About this thing, I have pleaded with the Lord three times for it to leave me, but he has said "My grace is enough for you; my power is at its best in weakness"'

St. Paul (2 Corinthians 12:8, 9)

BEYOND CRITICISM

READING 1 CORINTHIANS 2:10b–16
'The spiritual man judges all things, but is himself to be judged by no one. "For who has known the mind of the Lord so as to instruct him?" But we have the mind of Christ' (vv. 15, 16, RSV).

'Six feet above contradiction' is how the preachers' efforts are sometimes described. Many Christian pronouncements appear to take this line of approach. If it is God's Word for this generation, then surely it cannot be criticised. Verse 15 seems to encourage just such an attitude.

A partial way out of the difficulty is found in v. 16, about which John Hargreaves says 'We, not I. It is a fellowship of Christians rather than an individual to whom (according to this verse) God gives Himself.'

This is only a partial solution, for a community is only slightly less likely than an individual to be misguided about the degree to which they have the mind of God, in Christ. For as complete a solution as possible we need to return to v. 10b. **'For the Spirit searches everything, even the depths of God.'** In other words, no pronouncement is beyond criticism. Mature Christians will question the decisions and pronouncements of their leaders. They will consider them in the light of the gospel, praying for guidance as they do so.

Such criticism will not be made in order to achieve some political objective, or to score points over a rival. It will be made in order to come to a knowledge of the 'mind of Christ,' for Christ's mind, his will for us is made known *within* this world of conflict. 'We have received not the spirit of the world' (v. 12) – but we have received it in the world. We have received it powerfully, but still dimly. We need each others' honest ideas and criticisms in order to make that dim reflection clearer.

Let criticism be made, and taken in charity.   A PRAYER

MILK IS BABY'S FOOD

READING 1 CORINTHIANS 3:1–7,21–23; 4:6,7
'I fed you with milk, not solid food; for you were not ready for it; and even yet you are not ready, for you are still of the flesh. For while there is jealousy and strife among you, are you not of the flesh, and behaving like ordinary men?' (vv. 2,3, RSV).

The church in Corinth was four or five years old when Paul wrote. In that time he had expected development beyond the infant stage of baby milk. He expected his Corinthian readers to have progressed on to solid food, with a depth of spiritual life. Jealousy and wrangling, tensions and turbulence in the infant church should by now have been replaced by Christian charity and forbearance. Their infantile behaviour tried Paul's patience, so some of his words to the Corinthian congregation are quite harsh.

v. 4, see also 3 January

The rival factions seem to have been a bit like supporters' clubs, each shouting for their own player. Rivalry probably encouraged numerical growth, at the same time as discouraging spiritual depth.

Aware of the dangers of this supporter-club mentality, Paul stresses that in his own relationship with Apollos there is no rivalry. The potential for it was there, but it was not allowed to surface, or to find expression. What Paul preached, he practised.

It is difficult to associate a growing church with lack of spiritual depth, but it is an ever-present danger. Wherever personalities and powers are emphasised, that risk becomes a reality. May church growth never occur from rivalry, but through careful, Spirit-filled co-operation.

A PRAYER   *Where growth occurs may it always be greeted with charity, not jealousy.*

PICTURES, PICTURES, PICTURES

READING 1 CORINTHIANS 3:7–17
'Fellow workers for God; you are God's field, God's building . . . you are God's temple and . . . God's Spirit dwells in you' (vv. 9,16, RSV).

Paul does not tell stories like Jesus did. The most we get is a vivid comparison of the Christian with some specific object, a little word picture perhaps, which illustrates some aspect of the Christian life. We have three of them in this passage, field, building and temple (a particular kind of building). None is a complete picture, but each contributes something to the appreciation of the Christian's life and task.

The field picture may reflect Paul's knowledge of the parable of the sower, in which Jesus compares the people with different kinds of soil. Paul complicates the picture slightly, by comparing himself with a sower, and Apollos with one who waters the field, respectively. But notice how he describes the two tasks as equal.

The evangelist's task, the spectacular preaching may be more glamorous.

The pastor's task, the everyday care is of equal importance.

His building illustration is a little harder, for he gives the impression that we are responsible for our own building upon the Christian foundation which is laid. There is, however, a little let-out clause (v. 15), which shows that whatever our *works* are, they do not earn us our salvation. Paul's special contribution is to make us aware that we are God's temple, his special dwelling place, holy and usable.

PRAYER SUBJECT: *For a proper, Christian attitude to our physical body.*

PRAYER: *I would be thy holy temple,*
Sacred and indwelt by thee;

(Brindley Boon)

Lord, make me fit to be your temple. Help me to value my body, however frail it may be, so that others may see your Spirit, shining out from your own creation.

PAUL'S ARROGANCE?

READING 1 CORINTHIANS 4:1–5,8–13

'With me it is a very small thing that I should be judged by you or by any human court. I do not even judge myself. I am not aware of anything against myelf, but I am not thereby acquitted' (vv. 3,4, RSV).

In chapter 4, Paul is speaking from a lofty height. He is, according to John Ruef, 'trying to establish his apostolic authority.' We are shown the difficulties that apostleship entailed. Whatever the congregation might think about him, they need to take notice of what he is going to say. They may revile him for his stupid behaviour in becoming an apostle at all. But whatever their attitude to him, they must take notice of his words, not because of his desire to have authority over them, but because he wants them to receive a full, pure and powerful gospel.

v. 3   His contempt for human courts may sound arrogant, but needs to be set against his complete humility before God. He knows that even his own clear conscience is no guarantee of salvation. He depends entirely on God's mercy.

In today's world Paul would not be running for office, though he would encourage Christians who did. Christians of all political colours! He would not waste his energies opposing communism, or denouncing capital-

v. 13   ism. He would rather call for renewal in the Church, for reconciliation, for an appreciation of the riches of the

v. 8   gospel, not the riches of this world. Only when the Church takes such messages to its own heart can it begin to speak to those outside its borders with the clear, auth-oritative voice of its apostolic forbears.

LETTER FIRST, THEN AN EXAMPLE

READING 1 CORINTHIANS 4:14–17; 16:10
'I became your father in Christ Jesus through the gospel. I urge you, then, be imitatotors of me. Therefore I sent to you Timothy, my beloved and faithful child in the Lord, to remind you of my ways in Christ, as I teach them everywhere in every church' (vv. 15b–17, RSV).

The phrase 'When Timothy comes . . .' makes it seem Timothy was going to come to Corinth one day. The expression here 'I sent Timothy' makes it appear Timothy had already been. Most probably what happened was that Paul heard of difficulties in Corinth and sent Timothy overland to deal with the situation. Then, either because he heard of more difficulties, or because he wanted to help Timothy with his mission, Paul sent a letter by sea. The letter would get there before his young ambassador. By land the journey was about ten days, by sea, just three or four.

16:10

v. 17

Paul knew Timothy's worth, and the power of his example. He also knew how volatile the Corinthian congregation was, and the difficulty a young person faces when he tries to give advice, assert authority (albeit someone else's authority) or provide an example.

1 Tim 4:12

Samuel Johnson said that 'more people require to be reminded than instructed.' Paul, by sending the letter, reminded people that they needed to reconsider what they had already been taught and also gave added weight to Timothy's message. People are reminded of the gospel in many different ways.

We are taught to love the Lord,
We are taught to read his word,
We are taught the way to Heaven
Praise for all to God be given.
(John Henley)

LIBERTINES

READING 1 CORINTHIANS 4:18–5:8
'And you are proud! . . . Your boasting is not good' (vv. 2,6, NIV).

Ch. 1   Libertines, was the term we used for the Paul party. They felt that freedom in Christ was freedom to do exactly what they liked. As with so many groups, what they practised was very different from what was intended by the one they claimed to follow. Paul had no sympathy for 'libertine' views.

     Some centuries later Augustine said 'Love God and do as you like,' then qualified his statement to make it obvious that if you loved God truly, you would like what God wanted from you, rather as in Edwin Hatch's lovely verse

> Breathe on me, breath of God,
> Fill me with life anew,
> That I may love what thou dost love,
> And do what thou wouldst do.

     It is only when we have a deep, constant and humble relationship with God that we can approach the standard of Augustine's dictum 'Love God and do as you like.' The Corinthian Christians – and I dare say most of us – fall far short of that ideal. They, indeed, fell so far short that 'doing as they liked' involved acceptance of low moral standards that no reasonable society could tolerate. Arrogantly they claimed their libertine attitude was right.

     Paul's advice to turn the sexual offender over to Satan may seem harsh. It meant the offender should be excluded from the Christian fellowship. Once outside he would realise what he was missing, and repentance would be possible. Christian fellowships should be inclusive. Excluding anyone is a very serious matter, only to be resorted to in extreme circumstances.

A PRAYER   *We bring before you, Lord, all those who are excluded from Christian fellowship. May your Spirit reach out to them.*

A PREVIOUS LETTER

READING 1 CORINTHIANS 5:9–13
'When I wrote to you before I said not to mix with evil people. But when I said that I wasn't talking about unbelievers who live in sexual sin, or are greedy cheats and thieves or idol worshippers. For you can't live in this world without being with people like that' (vv. 9,10, LB).

Although the New Testament contains only two Corinthian letters, v. 9 shows there was a letter before 'first' Corinthians.* Paul also wrote a 'severe letter', making four in all.

see 2 Cor.
2:4

The first letter probably dealt with similar matters to those found in Ch. 5. Paul's advice was not to associate with immoral people. The Corinthians thought he meant 'Be separate from the world.' Elsewhere Paul does, indeed, say Christians must not follow the world's ways **'Don't copy the behaviour and customs of this world, but be a new and different person' (Romans 12:2).** But he does not ask Christians to live apart from the world. Christian holy living involves being in the world. There is a dilemma here. Holiness basically means 'separation.' But it must be separation *within* the world, not *from* the world. Holy living cannot be a merely individual matter. Paul's words are to the community at Corinth.

W. E. Sangster wrote 'The suggestion that religion is a purely individual concern, having no relation to the economic and political framework of society is offensive to our judgment and to our deepening religious thought. It assumes that, even if God did send his Son into the world to redeem the world, the world, through Him, will not be saved.' That, I suggest, gets at the heart of the 'Social Gospel' – a gospel with which Paul would readily identify.

TO PONDER

*Some scholars believe a fragment of the earlier letter is preserved in a passage from 2 Corinthians. Read today's passage then 2 Corinthians 6:11–7:4. They relate very well to each other, and 2 Corinthians 6:11–7:4 does seem to fit oddly in its present context. Whether the scholars' guess is right, we simply cannot be sure.

SCANDALS GALORE

READING 1 CORINTHIANS 5:13–6:11
'To have lawsuits at all with one another is defeat for you. Why not rather suffer wrong?' (v. 7, RSV).

Paul was no stranger to scandal. His advice in this chapter, that Christians should suffer wrong rather than go to law with each other may seem like hopeless idealism, but it is based on wide experience. We must abide by our own country's legal system, and churches cannot be exempt from things like charity laws; company regulations where they engage in commercial activities; employment regulations, and the like. But nothing makes more of a laughing-stock of the Church than the sight of its own members bickering with each other and, worse still, fighting things out in the law courts.

The Salvation Army had its own bitter experience of this in the legal wrangling which surrounded the first High Council in 1929, when there was a dispute over how a new General was to be chosen. Recovery took many years and old wounds remained for a generation. Many readers can doubtless think of other examples from their own church or chapel background.

Ecclesiastical courts, however, have also earned themselves a bad name over the centuries, so advice to settle within the judgment of the church would also be suspect. Beyond his words in v. 5, to seek advice from a wise Christian when there is a matter of dispute, Paul does not go. He has no blueprint for setting up church courts. In these days, where societies operate on a scale undreamt of in Paul's day, it is not always possible to take his advice literally. Sometimes legal definition is required. But . . .

TO PONDER   *Christians should think carefully, and read 1 Corinthians 5 even more carefully, before embarking on legal action against another, within or without the church.*

SEXUAL SCANDALS

READING 1 CORINTHIANS 6:12–20
' "All things are lawful for me," but not all things are helpful . . . Do you not know that your bodies are members of Christ?' (vv. 12,15, RSV).

Sexual scandals, especially if they involve members of the body of Christ, are part and parcel of the world's entertainment. Drives and instincts to which we are all subject, are the raw material of much of the world's drama. We study the incredible insights which certain playwrights and artists have into the deepest recesses of the human mind, and find them entertaining at the same time.

Sometimes this is a valuable exercise. Sometimes it helps reassure us we are not alone in experiencing deep, physical and emotional feelings. Sometimes it may enable us to appreciate that others feel in ways very different from our own instinctive orientations. However, all too often it becomes mere titillation, pandering to the lowest common denominator of physical desires.

What care we must take over how we channel bodily desires and instincts! All are God-given, and can be used in his service, but each one of them can also be corrupted. Sexual desire and its fulfilment are an integral part of the closest human relationship, marriage – but uncontrolled sexuality causes some of the most bestial crimes against those least able to defend themselves, particularly women and children. Paul's picture of the body as a temple of the Holy Spirit will not eradicate every sexual abuse overnight. But for members of the body of Christ, yesterday's last sentence can be adapted, albeit slightly awkwardly, to today's need.

v. 19

Christians should think carefully, and read 1 Corinthians 6 even more carefully, before embarking on any sexual relationship with another, within or without the church.

TO PONDER

NOW CONCERNING . . . (I) YOUR PROBLEMS

READING 1 CORINTHIANS 7:1–16,29–31
'The wife's body does not belong to her alone but also to her husband. In the same way, the husband's body does not belong to him alone but also to his wife' (v. 4, NIV).

Timothy and Titus are usually called 'The Pastoral Epistles.' First Corinthians is also pastoral, in great part written to answer specific difficulties outlined by the young church. Five times Paul answers with the words *Peri de* 'now concerning'. The infant church's first question was concerning physical relationships within marriage, then (RSV)

> At 7:25 'Now concerning the unmarried . . .'
> At 8:1   'Now concerning food offered to idols'
> At 12:1 'Now concerning spiritual gifts'
> At 16:1 'Now concerning the contribution for the saints'

Each was a pressing problem. Today's problems are different, but Paul's principles still apply. In keeping with the views of his Jewish contemporaries, Paul takes a very physical view of marriage. 'It is better to marry than to be aflame with desire'. When he wrote that he probably still believed the end of all things was close at hand (*see* 7:26,29). Only in such a context do some of his words make sense.

But note carefully his words in v. 4. The *NIV* brings out the sense most clearly. However physical or spiritual a marriage relationship may be, it is a relationship of equals. Each has equal responsibility to make it work.

PRAYER SUBJECT: *For true equality between the sexes.*
PRAYER: *We confess, Lord, it is hard for us not to put value judgments on differences. Help us never to regard anyone different from ourselves as inferior. Enable us to value the contributions made by people of both sexes to the common life of humanity. Guard us from extremes of both male chauvinism and militant feminism.*

CHRISTIAN FATALISM – PAULINE STYLE

READING 1 CORINTHIANS 7:17–24
'Was any one at the time of his call uncircumcised? Let him not seek circumcision . . . Were you a slave when called? Never mind . . . For he who was called in the Lord as a slave is a freedman of the Lord. Likewise he who was free when called is a slave of Christ' (vv. 18b,21a,22, RSV).

These verses seem to have an almost Hindu fatalism about them. Accept your station in life as assigned by God. Again it helps to look at the problems Paul was addressing. We know from other sources that it was fashionable for Hellenised Jews* to try and get rid of the marks of circumcision. We also know that there was constant pressure on new Christians to accept Jewish Law, including circumcision.

Acts 15:1

Both slavery and circumcision (or un-circumcision) were, in a sense, handicaps. They categorised people as outside the norm. Paul says 'Don't worry about either.' He encourages people to accept their own worth, in gospel terms he encourages them to 'love themselves' so that they can then love others.

Rich or poor, slave or free, male or female, white or black, able-bodied or handicapped. We are all both slaves and freedmen of the Lord. This is not a charter for oppression, but for freedom. No longer concerned about our own status, we become free. We can fight on our own behalf objectively. We can fight for other people without looking over our shoulders, or worrying about the reactions of society. May God give us that kind of freedom today.

> *Make me a captive, Lord,*
> *And then I shall be free*
> *Force me to render up my sword,*
> *And I shall conqueror be.*
> *(George Matheson)*

*Hellenised = Influenced by Greek culture.

NOW CONCERNING . . . (II) THE UNMARRIED

READING 1 CORINTHIANS 7:25–28,32–40
'Now concerning the unmarried, I have no word of the Lord, but I give my opinion as one who by the Lord's mercy is trustworthy' (v. 25, RSV).

The problems continue. Paul's view of this situation is, as we mentioned on Sunday, coloured by his expectation of the imminent coming of Christ. It is also coloured by his own commitment, and single state. As with everything he says, there is truth in it. Mutual obligations entered into by marriage partners do mean that their time and energy will be much occupied by each other. A single person can much more readily be dedicated to a cause, giving of time and talents.

11 January

20 January

26 January

However, in our study so far we have often come across the idea of the gospel relating to us in community. Paul was inadequate *on his own*. God gives himself to a *fellowship* of Christians. Jesus came to redeem *the world*. Even the single Christian is caught up in nets of fellowship, mutual ties, obligations, and is responsible to and for others in a different, but equally meaningful way.

Dietrich Bonhoeffer writes
'There is no single life which cannot experience the situation of responsibility; every life can encounter this situation in its most characteristic form, that is to say, in the encounter with other people. Even when free responsibility is more or less excluded from a person's vocational and public life, he/she nevertheless always stands in a responsible relation to other people . . . Where person meets person . . . there arises genuine responsibility.'

TO PONDER *Single or married, we are all equally responsible for our fellows, and need to cultivate love and concern for their needs which may at times appear to conflict with our dedication to 'the cause'.*

NOW CONCERNING . . . (III) LEGALISTS

READING 1 CORINTHIANS 8 (also 10:19,20,25–30)
'Now concerning food offered to idols . . . we know that "an idol has no real existence," and that "there is no God but one"' (vv. 1a,4b, RSV).

'Legalists' was the term we used for the Peter party. Chapters 8–11 seem to be addressed to those who want specific rules and regulations laid down, and those who want to 'sit in judgment' on Paul, in other words, legalists. We said Paul himself was no libertine. So, too, Peter himself was no legalist, and would probably have condemned the use of his name as a banner for this particular division within the church. `Ch. 1` `9:3 NIV` `25 January` `1 Pet. 1:22`

Elsewhere Paul makes it clear that there is no need to be fussy about where your food comes from. There are two things to bear in mind `Rom. 14`

1. **Act according to your own conscience.** A lovely line drawing which hangs in the hallway of our house portrays the faces of a number of different kinds of people. Around these very varied faces runs the phrase 'Each according to the dictates of his own conscience.' It is almost a standing family joke that 'Dad thinks that is a dangerous saying.'

2. **Moderate your conscience** according to the needs of your weaker brethren, so that their consciences are not offended by your actions (v. 11).

H. D. Lewis says, 'The voice of God is above all the voice of conscience, but not in the sense that it is nothing but one's conscience; it is a divine refinement of the working of conscience.' Without 'divine refinement' one's conscience may, indeed, be weak or even defiled. `TO PONDER` `v. 10` `v. 7`

THE PREACHER'S PRIVILEGE

READING 1 CORINTHIANS 9:1–18 (1–4,13–18)
'The Lord has commanded that those who preach the gospel should receive their living from the gospel. But I have not used any of these rights' (vv. 14,15a, NIV).

Have you noticed how vast numbers of plays and films feature the lives of actors and/or film stars? Playwrights and screen writers know about acting. Such works often contain a realism lacking when they cover subjects outside the acting world. It is natural to write about what you are familiar with. Paul was a preacher, an evangelist. It is natural he should write about the preacher's task, his rights, privileges and difficulties.

These 18 verses are passionate and repetitive, hence the suggestion that we could omit vv. 5–12 without losing too much of what Paul is trying to say.

v. 14   The rewards of preaching are not monetary. 'Receiving a living' must never be equated with high salary. It is 'a living,' and no more. Any highly paid preacher must naturally be suspect. Like most people Paul expected others to be grateful for the sacrifices he made on their behalf. Like many people, he was disappointed. But diappointment did not prevent him continuing in the same way, continuing to work for his living, as well as to preach. His reward was simply the newly awakened people of Corinth who had accepted the gospel.

Today an increasing number of 'worker priests,' evangelists and others support themselves in the way Paul did. Let us pray that their ministry will be effective, that their involvement in the work place will be positive, and that their contribution to the life of the church at large will be heeded.

TO PRAY   *Worker priests.*
ABOUT

ALL THINGS TO ALL MEN

READING 1 CORINTHIANS 9:19–23
'I have become all things to all men so that by all possible means I might save some' (v. 20, NIV)

This is one of those Scripture passages which can be misused to excuse all manner of injustice, double-dealing, compromise, dishonesty, hypocrisy, and hosts of other vices, on the grounds of 'identifying with the people I am working to save.' It is therefore doubly important to interpret it in the light of other passages, and not in isolation.

1. Paul is not committed to any one group within or without the church. He is free to act according to his own conscience, without glancing over his shoulder to his paymasters, or having all the time to think of the reaction of his friends. Before we can be 'all things to all men' we have to free ourselves of undue commitment to any particular group of people. Jesus loved the Samaritans, and pleaded their cause, but he did not claim to *be* one. (v. 19; John 9:48)

2. Freedom in the gospel is not licence. We may become Jews to win Jews, or weak to win the weak – even perhaps strong to win the strong, but can we become thieves to win the thief? Only in so far as we share their suffering. Jesus himself went to the cross with thieves, without himself being one. We may endure the conditions of the sinner as Jesus did, and risk being tainted by the sin. But we also have God's assurance that, whenever we act from love of our fellow men, then he is there. He identifies with us, saving us in the world, amongst both weak and strong.

A PRAYER

O Christ, who died with arms outstretched in love
For all who lift their faces to thy cross,
Fill, thou, our lives with charity divine,
Till thou and thine are all, and self is lost.
(Catherine Bonnell Arnott)

JOGGERS BEWARE?

READING 1 CORINTHIANS 9:24–27
'I do not run aimlessly . . . but I pommel my body and subdue it, lest after preaching to others I myself should be disqualified' (v. 27, RSV).

v. 24

Today's passage again requires careful interpretation, e.g. jogging could be seen as 'running aimlessly,' for there is no prize at the end of a simple jog. But it's quite obvious that's not what is in Paul's mind at all. He is not condemning jogging! Similarly, his idea that there is only one prize in a race cannot mean the Christian's prize is only going to one person – the logical conclusion of v. 24! Once more his illustration lacks the devastatingly simple quality of Jesus' parables.

v. 27

But we do well to meditate on the pommelling and subduing of the body. We do this, not to try to achieve salvation through self denial, but to remind ourselves that preaching the gospel is not an automatic ticket to paradise. Paul agrees wholeheartedly with Jesus when he says 'Many will say to me "Lord, Lord, did we not . . . do many mighty works in your name? And then I will declare to them "I never knew you; depart from me, you evil-

Matt. 7:22,23

doers"'.

22 January

Paul was very interested in the physical body. We have already seen he regarded it as a temple of God, even

2 Cor. 12:7

though his own body caused him much difficulty. Something made him very sensitive to the need for parts of the body to work together. Perhaps his own poor co-

Gal. 6:11,
'See with
what large
letters I am
writing'

ordination or failing eyesight. He was acutely aware of pain, and of the wholeness of the body. The rest of his letter is concerned with that wholeness as it relates to the living church. May we gain inspiration by accompanying him in his task of trying to unite the fragmented body of Christ in Corinth – or rather in twentieth century _____ where we live.

A PRAYER

Bind us together, Lord, bind us together in love.

READING 1 CORINTHIANS 10:1–13
'All were baptised into Moses . . . all ate the same supernatural food . . .
No temptation has overtaken you that is not common to man. God is
faithful, and he will not let you be tempted beyond your strength, but
with the temptation will provide a way of escape' (vv. 2,3,13, RSV).

The 'Christ party' were one of the factions at Corinth (17 January).
This passage is probably for them. They thought that they alone had
access to Christ himself, and that just for them 'the sacraments of
the church acted in a supernatural way. They claimed that they did
not have to worry about the natural results of their immoral activities'
(John Drane, Paul, Lion Publishing). Against these ideas Paul points
out that every Hebrew in the time of the Exodus had the same
experiences – baptism, i.e. rescue from the Red Sea – supernatural
food i.e., the manna provided daily. And all suffered the dire
consequences of the immorality of a few! (v. 8).

This does not mean that the necessary result of immorality is
immediate death – though the long and painful deaths resulting not
only from AIDS, but also in the past from syphilis and similar
diseases, do give us pause for thought. It is saying no one is immune
from the consequences of their actions. No 'Christ party' can claim
to be immune from ordinary physical limitations.

Similarly, no group is immune from temptation. Every temptation,
however deep and depraved it appears, is shared by others. None
is unique to you, or me! That is plain, but what Paul means by no
temptation coming to us which is beyond our strength to bear, is
more difficult. Any temptation we succumb to seems, surely, to be
too strong for us. Some are so completely destroyed by succumb-
ing to temptation that they almost cut off their own way of escape
and risk committing the 'sin against the Holy Spirit.' (Mark 3:29)

PRAYER SUBJECT: Those tempted 'beyond endurance'.
PRAYER: We confess, Lord, that it is hard to believe we are never
beyond your care. It is almost impossible in some situations to see
the way of escape provided. When we are weakest, when we feel
furthest away from you, remind us of your presence in ways that only
you know how.

SCANDALS OF DIVISION – I

READING 1 CORINTHIANS 10:14–21
'The cup of blessing, . . . the bread which we break, is it not a participation in the body of Christ? Because there is one bread, we who are many are one body, for we all partake of the one bread' (vv. 16,17, RSV).

The overall title of this study of 1 Corinthians is 'A Fragmented Church.' We have seen many different viewpoints being commented on by Paul. He has had strong words for those who take their own views to extremes at both ends of the religious spectrum.

In the fellowship of Christ it is possible for individuals with very different points of view, with very varied sensitivity and conscience to come together. The most tangible, visible symbol of this coming together is found in the Eucharist, the communion service where all partake of the physical bread. Some Corinthians took part in the communion, and also in similar pagan feasts. Their argument was probably – if I don't recognise that the idol or god has any real existence, then the feast means nothing to me, and can do no harm. Paul has already touched on this. Here he makes a further point that, whether the idol is real or not, all idol worship is demonic diverting people away from the truth, and so should be avoided.

Ch. 8
(1 February)

v. 20

Today's idols are more subtle, but everything which takes our attention away from God is, potentially, damaging.

A PRAYER

The dearest idol I have known,
Whate'er that idol be,
Help me to tear it from thy throne
And worship only thee.

(William Cowper)

THANK GOODNESS FOR GREEK SCHOLARS!

READING 1 CORINTHIANS 10:31–11:16
'I want you to understand that the head of every man is Christ, the head of a woman is her husband, and the head of Christ is God' (v. 3, RSV).

D. E. H. Whiteley *The Theology of St. Paul*, tells us that *cephale*, translated 'head' in most English versions, actually meant 'source' in pre-Biblical Greek. We can see that this is also in Paul's mind. Compare v. 8 with the creation story in Genesis 2, and we gain some idea of the basic background of Paul's thinking. He sees woman as coming from man, i.e. man is the source from which woman is derived, though his comment in v. 11 should also be read!

v. 8

Soldier's Armoury 2/3 December 1988

He is not so much concerned here with authority – which is what 'head' implies. He is concerned about what is proper and seemly. In Corinth, as in other Greek cities, women without head-coverings who took part in religious services could be only one thing, cult prostitutes. To avoid any such misunderstanding occurring, Paul advises Christian women to cover their heads.

To add force to his words he searches for Biblical authority for what he says. We all do it. Paul was no exception. To clinch an argument we try to support *our* view from the Bible. This is the wrong way round. Rather let us allow the Bible to speak to us, and affect the views we have. *Our* ideas come from a different background, so it takes careful thought to make best use of the varied Biblical material. It also means it is often impossible to apply Scriptural regulations to today's situations directly. What we can do is look at the principles involved, and go on from there, humbly and prayerfully.

v. 8

The Spirit is needed for the understanding of Scripture and every part of Scripture.

A THOUGHT

(Martin Luther)

SCANDALS OF DIVISION – II

READING 1 CORINTHIANS 11:17–22,33,34
'When you meet together, it is not the Lord's supper that you eat' (v. 20, RSV).

It would appear that the custom at Corinth, at least before they received Paul's letter, was to celebrate the communion service as a full meal, just as the Last Supper was a full meal. The church at Corinth was poor. Presumably it was difficult to provide a set meal for everyone, so the congregation brought their own.

Unfortunately this highlighted economic divisions within the community. Some had plenty, others little or nothing. What an opportunity to share! But the opportunity was missed. Paul in his wisdom probably realised such sharing was practically impossible. Instead he advised them to celebrate communion as a symbolic meal, simply remembering Jesus' actions at the last supper.

Paul's advice to the Corinthian Christians solved the outward problem of scandalous division between rich and poor at the communion table. It did not solve the wider problem of the scandalous difference between rich and poor in the Christian community at large. That is still a scandal which should weigh heavily on the heart of each and every Christian.

Nor did Paul anticipate later theological divisions which would divide Christians of different backgrounds (denominations), making some unwelcome to partake of the bread and wine because of those differences. Although there is a long way to go before full inter-communion exists between all Churches, those differences are now being overcome, slowly but surely.

TO THINK
ABOUT

At a time when the scandalous gap between rich and poor countries is causing increasing concern, numbers of rich countries are reducing the tax 'burden' of rich individuals – thus increasing the gap between rich and poor in their own lands. Christians who remain silent about this are 'passing by on the other side'

Luke
10:31,32

A GREAT DIFFERENCE

READING 1 CORINTHIANS 11:23–32
'This careless participation . . . is the reason for the many sickly and feeble Christians in your church, and the explanation of the fact that so many of you are spiritually asleep' (v. 30, JBP).

One great difference between Salvationists and most Christian groups is that they have no communion service as part of their normal programme of worship. The reasons are many. The following, though by no means a complete statement, may help the majority of our readers, who are not Salvationists, to understand something of this unusual stance.

1. Historical accident, closely tied to pioneering an equal ministry for women. In the nineteenth century getting women accepted into the pulpit was hard enough. Acceptance of their administering the sacrament would have been well-nigh impossible!

2. Salvationists recognise fully the value in sacramental worship. They emphasise the spiritual nature of everything sacramental by their view that no specific ceremony (e.g. communion) is necessary to salvation. The same grace transmitted in the rite of communion is also transmitted through other forms of worship. Communion is not a magic rite. Its content is spiritual. 'Careless participation' is just as serious in those areas of prayer, Bible reading, singing, prophesying etc. as it is in the communion service.

3. The scandal of division. In earlier days salvationists were encouraged to take communion in their local churches. They found, however, that they were either welcome or not welcome according to which denomination had baptised them. Intercommunion is gradually overcoming such divisions.

PRAYER

Let us pray for the coming of the day when all divisions concerning celebration of the sacraments are overcome. May the Salvationists' emphasis on the spiritual nature of the sacrament contribute to, not detract from, unity.

NOW CONCERNING . . . (IV) SPIRITUAL GIFTS. SPIRITUAL PRIDE!

READING 1 CORINTHIANS 12:1–11
'No one speaking by the Spirit of God ever says "Jesus be cursed" and no one can say "Jesus is Lord" except by the Holy Spirit' (v. 3, RSV).

The early Church was persecuted, more strongly at some times than others, but always persecuted to some degree. The easiest way for a Roman judge to test if the accused was Christian, was to ask him or her to curse Jesus. If they refused it was an admission of guilt, and punishment followed – sometimes even to death.

However, some Christians tried to avoid the test by saying that if they uttered the curse without actually meaning it, then it was not a curse at all. In this they claimed to be led by the Spirit! They were, I suppose, the people who took 'libertine' ideas to the extreme.

25 January,
1 February

Even more remarkably some interpreters claim that this statement 'Jesus be cursed' was actually used by some Christians to prove their spirituality. These Christians felt they were so holy, so unaffected by normal everyday things, they could even say 'Jesus be cursed' without it damaging them spiritually. Paul condemned such attitudes so effectively that they sound silly today, but there are equally serious examples of spiritual pride to be found in today's church.

We can still find Christians who think themselves so holy that they cannot sin. We still find Christians who think that only they are right. We still find Christians who virtually curse Jesus in their hearts by their condescending attitude to others who think differently, or act differently from themselves. There is room in God's kingdom for all who acknowledge that 'Jesus is Lord' and who fully divest themselves of spiritual pride.

I want a principle within of jealous, Godly fear,
A sensibility of sin, a pain to feel it near.
(Charles Wesley)

MANY GIFTS, ONE SPIRIT

READING 1 CORINTHIANS 12:11–26
'The body does not consist of one member but of many . . . If one member suffers, all suffer together; if one member is honoured, all rejoice together' (vv. 14,26, RSV).

Ch. 12 is so closely knit together, with the same illustration sustained throughout, it seems impertinent even to think of splitting it. Today's passage needs setting alongside yesterday's. The nine gifts listed are not the vv. 8–10 only gifts of the Spirit. Others can be found in Romans 12. Even then we do not have a complete list. Those which Paul mentions by name are the most obvious, the ones on public display. But they are not necessarily the most essential.

In the ancient world similar pictures of the body were used by philosophers and politicians to pacify those of inferior status when they were tempted to revolt. Paul, however, uses the body illustration differently. As Jean Hering states, 'he is not so much afraid of a possible revolt of the inferior members, but of the pride of the "superior," who perhaps squabbled among themselves about the excellence of their respective gifts'. He also says 'this unity in diversity is an ordinary fact, which should neither puff up those who have received more outstanding gifts, nor discourage the others who do humble but equally necessary services to the Church'. William Baugh puts it differently but powerfully in his verse

> '*'Tis true I have no room to boast;
> When most I'm saved I'm humbled most;
> Kept low by grace and not by sin,
> My soul shall make her boast in Him.*

A MORE EXCELLENT WAY

READING 1 CORINTHIANS 12:26–13:3
'Earnestly desire the higher gifts. And I will show you a still more excellent way' (v. 31, RSV).

Gifts are a by-product of the Christian life, fine and desirable, but never the main aim. It's a hard lesson to learn. It can make Christianity unpopular, for many crave the gifts rather than the giver. Craving spiritual gifts is not wrong in itself, any more than sex is wrong in itself. But a wrongly directed urge to acquire even spiritual gifts can be as damaging as a wrongly directed sexual urge. If our desire to acquire spiritual gifts makes us envy those who already have them, it is being wrongly directed. Such desire is only healthy within a lasting, steady relationship with Jesus.

If the gift takes your mind away from the giver, something is wrong.

If it brings injury to other members of the body, something is wrong.

Follow the more excellent way, the way of love – the way of relationship with Jesus above all else and the gifts will fall into place. Michael Green's book *I Believe in the Holy Spirit* says 'We shall expect to see the work of the Spirit in the interdependence of the church membership, where love controls attitudes, and where gifts are used for the good of the community, not for the gratification of the individual . . . In the church where the Spirit is given freedom, the charismatic will not obtrude his gift, and the settled ministry will not fear it. Both strands need each other in the corporateness of the body of Christ; and both will, in the church where the Spirit is obeyed, resist the temptation of seceding from their sometimes awkward bedfellows.'

PRAYER SUBJECT: *For an outpouring of the Spirit in our community.*
PRAYER: *Thou Christ of burning, cleansing flame, send the fire!*
Thy Blood-bought gift today we claim. Send the fire!
Look down and see this waiting host,
Give us the promised Holy Ghost.
We want another Pentecost. Send the fire!

(William Booth)

THE SUPREMACY OF LOVE

READING 1 CORINTHIANS 13:4–13
'At present we see only the baffling reflections in a mirror, but then it will be face to face' (v. 12, JM).

Faith, hope and love are the three gifts which will remain, which are carried over from time into eternity. They are the supreme virtues. And they are closely interwoven with each other.

What is faith without hope and love?
  Just a cold, intellectual conviction with no saving
    power at all.
What is hope without faith and love?
  Just a dream, a bubble that will burst one day.
What is love without faith and hope?
  Just passion, just feeling, just emotion, without any
    principle or any foundation.
                                      (Alan Redpath)

If all three remain, what is it about love which causes it to surpass the others, and to be the supreme virtue? Surely it is *the* virtue which involves others. We can have our own faith. We can hold to our own hope in spite of everything around us. But love requires another. We cannot just love ourselves. It is also the virtue which, above all, we share with God himself. God does not have faith, he is the object of faith. God does not have hope, for he already knows. But he does have love. Indeed he is love.

        Love suffereth patiently, Love worketh silently
            Love seeketh not her own.
        Love never faileth, Love still prevaileth,
            Lord, in me thy love enthrone!
                                      (Arch R. Wiggins)

THE GIFT OF TONGUES

READING 1 CORINTHIANS 14:1–17
'Since you are eager for manifestations of the Spirit, strive to excel in building up the church' (v. 12, RSV).

More heat has been created and less light received in argument about this gift than any other. This particular gift is so remarkable, and relatively easy to experience, that it is all too easy to use it as a measure of a particular kind of blessedness – and some would even dare to suggest that without it one is an inferior kind of Christian. Many who are not blessed with the gift become worried about their lack of spirituality and many of those endowed with it become proud of theirs.

12:31

12 February

Here, more than anywhere, we need to heed Paul's words about 'a more excellent way' and the comments of Michael Green.

Acts 10:45 could give us the impression that speaking with tongues is an inevitable result of infilling by the Spirit. Paul, too, in today's passage, says he would like everyone to experience the gift. But the previous chapter shows how different gifts are given to different people, and no one should expect to have them all. Anyway, it is far more important that all should prophesy – and even that gift is not in fact open to all.

12:29

The gift of tongues is also terrifyingly easy to counterfeit. It can be used by the devil, or by quite neutral, non-Christian agencies. The speaker in a tongue who is under the control of the Spirit is also responsive to control by the leader of the meeting. Good order and 'building up the church' is the key to any use of this most remarkable gift.

PRAYER *Lord, help us to 'excel in building up the church' by every means you put at our disposal.*

BELIEVERS OR UNBELIEVERS?

READING 1 CORINTHIANS 14:18–33a
'Tongues are a sign not for believers but for unbelievers, while pro-phecy is not for unbelievers but for believers. If, therefore, the whole church assembles and all speak in tongues and outsiders or un-believers enter, will they not say that you are mad?' (vv. 22,23, RSV).

The apparent contradiction in today's passage is so great that J. B. Phillips' translation departs from the text found in all the manuscripts and assumes there is a copyist's error. His version of v. 22 runs 'Tongues are a sign of God's power, not for those who are unbelievers but for those who already believe.' How different from the *RSV* text above!

It is easy to understand how Phillips became so des-perate as to make the change. I, too, am often tempted to accept that here, uniquely, is an instance where the unanimous witness of all the manuscripts has to be ignored and a mistake recognised. Or do the following thoughts resolve the difficulty?

In Greek it is possible for the dative case, translated in most versions 'for unbelievers' to mean 'against unbelievers.' This is a simple solution, argued quite thoroughly in a learned article by J. P. M. Sweet some twenty years ago, but no modern translations have taken up the idea as it involves giving a forced technical sense to the original text.

Other commentators stress the fact that Paul's Old Testament quote is a very free translation, and the 'un-believers' are actually members of the community of God already. E.g. those unbelieving members of the com-munity who had to be spoken to by the strange tongues of the Assyrians. Their hearts had been hardened in a similar way to those of the crowds to whom Jesus spoke so often. The strange tongues were a judgement on the halfhearted. Public use of the gift of tongues is of little help in building up the community, and in this sense prophecy is needed for believers, rather than tongues.

Isa. 28:11

Matt. 13:14

WOMEN PROPHESYING, WOMEN SILENT

READING 1 CORINTHIANS 14:33b–40
'As in all the churches of the saints, the women should keep silence in the churches' (v. 33b,34a, RSV).

Today's apparent contradiction is much easier to resolve than yesterday's. Paul has already spoken about women prophesying. He speaks about it as an ordinary and accepted part of the well-ordered service in church. In Corinth they should pray or prophesy with their heads covered. We saw the reasons for that on January 24.

How then can Paul at the same time deny women the possibility of speaking in church? The answer is that he doesn't. By speaking, in this instance, he means either gossiping or public dissent. In the synagogue it was normal for a speaker to be challenged about his interpretation of the Law. Paul asks that such questioning should not be carried over into the Christian church service, at least not by the women. It is still very much a matter of culture. Women in Paul's day should not question the authority of men. But even in Paul's day they were not forbidden to prophesy or preach!

Catherine Booth, writing over a century ago states 'Whether the Church will allow women to speak in *her* assemblies can only be a question of time; common sense, public opinion and the blessed results of female agency will force her to give us an honest and impartial rendering of the solitary text on which she grounds her prohibitions. Then, when the true light shines and God's works take the place of man's traditions, the doctor of divinity who shall teach that Paul commands woman to be silent when God's spirit urges her to speak will be regarded much the same as we should regard an astronomer who should teach that the sun is the earth's satellite.' Mrs. Booth's prophecies are being fulfilled, but there is still a long way to go!

PRAYER SUBJECT
Women preachers who still have to overcome prejudice against them from within their own congregations.

THE FIRST WRITTEN WITNESS

READING 1 CORINTHIANS 15:1–11
**'Last of all he appeared to me too and my birth into the family of Christ
was as violent and unexpected as an abortion' (vv. 7,8, WB).**

Ch. 15 gives us a priceless insight into Paul's thoughts on
the resurrection. It is probably the earliest written witness
we have to that event, for First Corinthians circulated
before the gospels as we have them today were in their
final written form.

Although first into writing, Paul always regarded himself as last and least of the apostles. For his knowledge of
the events of the last supper, the crucifixion itself, and the
appearances of Christ to the disciples, Paul relied on the
tradition he had received from others. But he could make
his own witness to Christ's resurrection. Barclay's translation 'as violent and unexpected as an abortion' is a bit
extreme – but so was Paul's experience. We shall see the
full implications of that as our study of Ch. 15 continues.
At this stage simply note how Paul maintains a clear
balance between tradition on the one hand and personal
experience on the other. We need both.

Without the written, or spoken 'received' tradition an
experience may be meaningless. When Christ con-
fronted Paul on the Damascus road that did not suffice to
make Paul into a full-fledged apostle. First Ananias   Acts 9:10–19
taught him, then he went for three years into the desert to
study.   Gal. 1:17

For ordinary Christians: Sometimes we envy, Lord, those   A PRAYER
who have had startling revelations, blinding lights com-
ing to them, and wonderful confirmations of your calling
to them. We imagine it must be easier for them. Help us to
remember the experience of Paul. Make us aware of the
long years of effort, study and following in every adverse
circumstance. Thank you for the light we do have. Re-
move from us all envy of the light others have received.

THE CHURCH: THE BODY OF CHRIST

READING 1 CORINTHIANS 15:12–34
'If it is for this life only that Christ has given us hope, we of all men are most to be pitied' (v. 19, NEB).

The Church as the Body of Christ is central to Paul's thinking. Of course he recognises our individuality. Our salvation is strongly connected to individual belief and acceptance of Christ's way, the way of the cross. But Christian life is lived in community. That community, the Church in all its varied forms, is an imperfect body which is continually being transformed through the work of the Holy Spirit, and through the Spirit's transformation of the lives of individual Christians.

See
Rom. 12:2

Such transformation continues beyond the point of death. It is not complete here on earth. Denis Duncan writes 'it is clear that death is part of the journey to that wholeness which is completed in God's presence.' In more technical language, John Robinson writes

> 'The habit of treating 1 Corinthians 15 in isolation from the rest of Paul's writing has tended to obscure its connection with the very much larger number of passages which depict this gradual transformation and glorification of the body from baptism onwards. The result is that the final change has become mistakenly conceived as quasi-magical and unrelated to anything that has gone before'

We can now begin to understand v. 19 which appears so mournful at first. It seems to say Christians are miserable souls. Pity them if their hope of the next life is in vain, because their life here on earth is so miserable! But it is not saying that at all. It's saying Christians should be pitied if the transformation they experience here on earth does not continue. That is quite a different matter.

TO PONDER   *Death is a natural end and a natural beginning, part of a continual process of transformation which will be complete only after the day of judgment.*

DEATH: THE LAST ENEMY

READING 1 CORINTHIANS 15:35–49
'But some may ask, ''How are the dead raised? With what kind of body will they come? How foolish! What you sow does not come to life unless it dies' (vv. 35,36, NIV).

Death is the last enemy (*v. 26*), to be destroyed. But it is only an enemy in one particular sense. It emphasises our separation from God, brought about by Adam's sin. (*Genesis 3:19*) It marks the absolute gulf between God and Man. By bridging that gap, by both experiencing and conquering death, Jesus re-unites us with God. Our final reunion with God takes place the other side of death. What form will it take? Paul does not claim to know. He lives in hope.

Our frail, imperfect, earthly bodies could not stand the impact of reunion with God. Paul says there is more difference between our present, earthly body and the future, heavenly one than between a seed and the flower, fruit or tree which it produces. Or, put another way, more difference than between the egg in a woman's ovary and a fully-grown human being.

In Paul's day continuity from seed to flower was not as clear as it is to us. They appear radically different, but we know there is real continuity between seed and flower. Similarly there is real continuity between the earthly and resurrection body, even though the difference is also greater.

Read again yesterday's quote from Denis Duncan. The modern hospice movement takes such ideas seriously. It exists in order to ensure that people facing the reality of death will have a 'good' death. It witnesses to the fact that there is 'a healing through dying.'

PRAYER SUBJECT: *The hospice movement.*

PRAYER: *Thank you, Lord, for healers who dedicate their lives to caring for the dying. Thank you for hospices which ease the passage from life to death. Help all who work in them to cope positively with the pressures that arise from such continual care. May personal and state financial resources be made available to aid them in their God-given task.*

RESURRECTION AND IMMORTALITY

READING 1 CORINTHIANS 15:50–58
'"Death has been swallowed up in victory." "Where, O death, is your victory? Where, O death, is your sting?" The sting of death is sin, and the power of sin is the law. But thanks be to God! He gives us the victory through our Lord Jesus Christ' (vv. 54b–57, NIV).

v. 54

Christian doctrine does not stress immortality of the soul. Christian doctrine speaks about resurrection. It says 'the perishable has been clothed with the imperishable, and the mortal with immortality.' In other words, as with salvation, it is by God's grace and favour that we enjoy the resurrection. It is God who is victorious over sin and death. And he passes that victory on to us.

Eph. 1:14,
2 Cor. 1:22

In doing so he changes us. The change begins in this life and we enjoy a taste of the joys to come. But it is only a taste. It is not the whole meal. John Short writes 'God in Christ is working in us . . . investing us with the very quality and spirit of eternal life. We are being fashioned, slowly it may be, with "many a labour, many a sorrow, many a tear," into Christlikeness. We are being fashioned in "the image of the man of heaven," the greatest of all personalities. Our personal life and quality, as we follow him in sincerity and truth and love are being progressively enriched.'

v. 56

We can fairly easily understand that 'the sting of death is sin'. Without sin, death holds no fears. Jesus' own fear of death was surely because of the weight of man's sin, and his own sense of separation from God. It was simply part of his human existence. But to say that the power of sin is the law seems very hard. Elsewhere Paul says the

Rom. 7:12,
Gal. 3:21

Law is good, yet at the same time it is only because the law is there that we know we are sinning. Such is the law's power. It gives knowledge of sin, and thus unleashes the power of sin. How necessary for us to be transformed by the power of God to enable us to overcome both sin and the power of the Law.

A THOUGHT *Knowledge is power – for good or ill.*

READING 1 CORINTHIANS 16:1–4
'On the first day of every week, each one of you should set aside a sum of money in keeping with his income, saving it up, so that when I come no collections will have to be made' (v. 2, NIV).

When Paul gives instruction or advice that sounds 'theological' or 'doctrinal' there is a tendency to treat it as THE word for all ages, and perhaps ignore the context. When he gives financial advice we naturally interpret it according to context. No one would dream of claiming that as v. 2 says put aside a sum on the first day of every week and save it up until Paul comes, then Sunday church collections for general upkeep are unscriptural! Paul's advice is good and sound. Set aside part of your income every week for the support of God's people, but the special instruction we naturally interpret as applying only to the Corinthian situation and related to Paul's anticipated visit.

In the same way, we can't say that because Paul's request is for the Jerusalem church, then we too should do the same. Some may feel called to support the work of Christ in the Holy Land, but not all. Paul's words do, however, remind us of the need to support the work of Christ financially as well as by our presence with other Christians in worship.

Note that Paul asks an impoverished church in which 'not many were influential' to help another church. Some years ago there was an earthquake in Italy. The Salvation Army was one of the agencies involved in relief work. Some women salvationists in Mizoram, a remote corner of Eastern India, heard about this and immediately sent a gift to help in the work of reconstruction. That gift, though not large in monetary terms was a great morale booster. It inspired those who worked there. It is recorded here for you and thousands of other *Words of Life* readers, in the hope that it inspires you, both to give yourselves, and to appreciate gifts that are given.

1 Cor. 1:26

FURTHER
READING
SUGGES-
TION

Mark 12:41–44

PAUL'S PASTORAL WORK

READING 1 CORINTHIANS 16:5–14
'I do not want to see you now and make only a passing visit. I hope to spend some time with you if the Lord permits' (v. 7, NIV).

1 Thess.
1:17; 2 Cor.
1:15

Phil. 4:1

Eph.
1:18–19

Paul's pastoral activity was not just a case of one visit, then leave the new church to its own devices. Some of his pastoral correspondence with new churches has come down to us, like the letter we are studying. But he also made extended visits, and always wanted to have more time with individual churches, to nurture them in the faith; to keep up old acquaintances and friendships; and try to ensure that they kept Christ central in their thinking.

2 Cor. 2:1

Acts 20:3

After sending 1 Corinthians, Paul received bad news about the Church and had to make a 'painful visit' to them, which is not recorded in Acts. However, later on he did spend the winter in Corinth with the church there. We must assume from this, and from the joyful tone of much of 2 Corinthians, that his pastoral care of this fragmented and tension-filled community did finally bear the fruit of reconciliation. Study of the rest of Paul's Corinthian correspondence in *Words of Life* must wait till a later date, but this is an opportune time to study again the notes on that correspondence made at the beginning of our study.

Pastoral activity like Paul's, takes effort, vast amounts of energy and time. It makes great demands on an individual who takes up the task. And, it can only be done with support from other Christians. A pastor, unsupported by his congregation, is in a perilous position indeed. He needs friends and helpers like Timothy and Apollos. Sometimes pliable and obedient as Timothy; sometimes less easily swayed, like Apollos who fitted his ministry on Paul's behalf into his own schedule. But each in his own way supported. Sensitive pastors will use both kinds of support, and many others.

LET US
PRAY

That pastors will always find help within a living, vibrant church in 1989.

BLESSINGS, A CURSE AND DIFFERENT WORDS FOR LOVE

READING 1 CORINTHIANS 16:15–24
'I, Paul, write this greeting in my own hand. If anyone does not love the Lord – a curse be on him. Come, O Lord' (vv. 21,22, NIV).

At the end of 1 Corinthians Paul sends warm, personal greetings and blessings from Ephesus, especially to Stephanus, Fortunatus and Achaicus. These men presumably acted as messengers, or perhaps came of their own accord to Paul because of their great concern over the serious problems facing their home church at Corinth. We don't, however, know the exact circumstances which brought them to Paul in Ephesus.

All of Paul's letters contain greetings. The one at the beginning of Galatians is unique, for it is the only one of Paul's letters which *starts* without a word of thanks. But the extra personal greeting which Paul adds in his own hand at the *end* of 1 Corinthians runs it a close second, and indeed contains the unique phenomenon of a curse! Paul seems to be asking for a curse on anyone who is not a Christian. God forbid!

The word he uses for 'love' is the key to his thought in this instance. Usually he uses the standard Christian word 'agape' but in this instance he uses the term 'philos'. It is almost as though he is saying 'you are cursed if you haven't even got the lower attitude of love for Christ that "philos" implies' – let alone the greater gift of Christian 'agape'. Once more his harshest words, like those of his Master, are for the halfhearted.

Luke
9:57–62

Lord I make a full surrender. All I have I yield to thee;
For thy love, so great and tender, asks the gift of me.
Lord, I bring my whole affection. Claim it take it for thine
*   own,*
Safely kept by thy protection, fixed on thee alone.
*   (Lowell L. Mason)*

FULL COM-
MITMENT

A SONG OF ASCENTS

READING PSALM 120
'Too long have I lived among those who hate peace.
I am a man of peace; but when I speak, they are for war' (vv. 6,7, NIV).

Fifteen psalms have the title 'A song of ascents'. Some scholars believe this indicates they were used in procession as the priests ascended the Temple steps. Others believe they are pilgrim psalms, used mainly by worshippers on their way to the great feasts in Jerusalem three times a year. The greatest was the Feast of Passover, which every Jew still celebrates, saying at the end 'And next year – in Jerusalem!'

It is a stirring thought that perhaps Jesus himself approached Jerusalem for that final Passover singing these Psalms. He identified with other pilgrims who came from all corners of the earth. They came from situations where often they were hated, for Jews stood out as righteous and God-fearing in a pagan world. How ironic that Jesus would be cut down by those very people who suffered so much from persecution themselves.

For most people the cry of v. 7 'I am a man of peace, but . . . they are for war' is an empty one. Few of us really turn the other cheek when faced by those who oppose or persecute us. But for Jesus, going on his way with his disciples to Jerusalem the cry of Psalm 120 v. 7 was true. Yet somehow I doubt if this particular Psalm would be uppermost in his mind, for the quality of those who really are for peace is that they get on with it, while so many of us, (like the psalmist himself?) simply *speak* of peace.

> *Too long mistrust and fear*
> *Have held our souls in thrall;*
> *Sweep through the earth, keen breath of heaven*
> *And sound a nobler call!*
> *Come as thou didst of old,*
> *In love so great that men*
> *Shall cast aside all other gods*
> *And turn to thee again.*

(John Oxenham)

HELP FROM THE HILLS?

READING PSALM 121
'I will lift up mine eyes unto the hills, from whence cometh my help'
(v. 1, AV).
'I lift up my eyes to the hills. From whence does my help come?'
(v. 1, RSV).

Today's psalm provides an example of the way that shallow Bible study may seriously damage spiritual health. For many years, like most other people, I thought Psalm 121 meant what it said. 'I will lift up my eyes to the hills, where my help comes from'.

It was easy to associate God with the hills. It was easy to think of God away beyond the undulating horizon, yet at the same time possible to contact when help was needed. I pictured the psalmist gaining inspiration from nature, and writing the beautiful words of Psalm 121 under that inspiration.

Imagine the shock when modern versions added a question mark to the first verse! 'Where does my help come from?' Fortunately the answer is still 'My help comes from God,' but it was not until Kenneth Taylor's 'Living Bible' was published that the reason for not looking to the hills became clear to me.

He translated v. 1 as follows **'Shall I look to the mountain gods for help? No! My help is from Jehovah.'** A shallow study of modern translations had led me to believe the psalmist was saying 'You must not try to gain inspiration from nature.' Knowledge of the background, a knowledge which Kenneth Taylor used in his paraphrase, shows that the psalmist is not talking about the inspiration we receive from nature, but is talking about the worship of gods of nature – a different thing entirely.

Do I use every means for worship which God puts at my disposal?

TO THINK ABOUT

THE PILGRIM'S PSALM

READING PSALM 122
'Pray for the peace of Jerusalem: May those who love you be secure. May there be peace within your walls and security within your citadels' (vv. 6, 7, NIV).

This psalm is the one out of all fifteen 'songs of ascents' which is most clearly associated with going up to Jerusalem for one of the feasts. We can imagine the pilgrims standing, looking down at Jerusalem across the valley. They notice how 'closely compacted' *(v. 3)* are its narrow streets and winding alleyways. Their thoughts would be mixed. For some it would be the excited fulfilment of a lifetime's dream, for others disappointment at the little, dusty, in-significant-looking city.

Throughout its history Jerusalem has been a troubled city. Today, if anything, more troubled than ever. We could say it is a barometer of the world situation – a city where one feels, if peace comes there, it is possible for peace to break out anywhere. Divisions between Arab and Jew, between Christians, Muslims and Jews are high-lighted there as nowhere else on earth. Yet still the pilgrims come; Christians by the tens of thousands, at Easter and Christmas especially; Jews at the great festivals; Muslims also on certain occasions coming to the Dome of the Rock. Friday prayers, the Sabbath day's rest and celebration of Sunday follow one upon the other in quick succession.

What an opportunity exists in Jerusalem for dialogue between religious groups. How seldom is that opportunity taken! Not until each group can say in the words of v. 9 'For the sake of the house of the Lord our God, I will seek your prosperity' i.e. the prosperity of all groups in the city, will any difference be found in the troubled affairs of Jerusalem.

PRAYER SUBJECT: *For those with whom we strongly disagree.*
A PRAYER: *Speak out the promise in v. 9. Apply it personally to a particular individual or group with whom you strongly disagree. Pray earnestly for their prosperity. It will be difficult. It will make a remarkable difference to you.*

SLAVERY IS A THING OF THE PAST

READING PSALM 123
'As the eyes of slaves look to the hand of their master, . . . so our eyes look to the Lord our God, till he shows us mercy' (v. 2, NIV).

Although poor and disadvantaged people the world over are still exploited by the unscrupulous, there is general agreement that it is not permissible for one human being to 'own' another, to buy and sell people, or keep them in conditions which amount to slavery.

Comparing our relationship with God to the relationship between a slave and his master is therefore bound to be unpopular. Most of us think we have grown beyond such a relationship. For others it has little meaning, simply because slavery is so much a thing of the past. Yet this phrase uncovers an important truth. Our dependence on God is as complete as that of a slave's dependence upon his master. Think what that means. It means we cannot ask God for anything as of right. We cannot say to God 'I have a right to live' or 'I have a right to prosperity'.

We simply come to him, thank him for what he has given, ask him for what we require, and pray that he will use us. It is all a question of His mercy, not of our own rights or demands.

John Wesley's translation of Joachim Lange's words may help our meditation.

> *Now, O my God, thou hast my soul,*   PRAYER
> *No longer mine, but thine I am;*
> *Guard thou thine own, possess it whole,*
> *Cheer it with hope, with love inflame.*
> *Thou hast my spirit, there display*
> *Thy glory to the perfect day.*

AN EVER PRESENT HELP

READING PSALM 124
'If the Lord had not been on our side when men attacked us, when their anger flared against us, they would have swallowed us alive' (vv. 2,3, NIV).

We have no means of telling the historical background to this psalm, or to Psalm 123. Yesterday we saw the little people of Israel being mocked by the proud and arrogant. The little tribe, or nation, felt such mockery keenly. Goliath the Philistine mocked them. Centuries later, in the time of Nehemiah, their enemies Sanballat, Tobiah and Geshem laughed them to scorn. Nor can we tell whether today's praise for victory stems from Egypt's humiliation at the time of the Exodus, from Goliath's defeat, from the staving off of attack in Isaiah's day, or the triumph over the same Sanballat, Tobiah and Geshem.

1 Sam. 17:8

Neh. 4:2,3

Exod. 14:24
1 Sam. 17:50
Isa. 37:36
Neh. 7:1

Countless occasions would fit, and on countless occasions we can see the question arising 'Whose side is the Lord on?' or the deeper question 'Does victory really mean the Lord is on our side?' For if it does, what then is meant by defeat? That the Lord has forsaken us? Time and again the Old Testament gives the answer 'No!' Time and again God's people are defeated, yet still the Lord is with them. Their survival is truly a miraculous story.

Why did they survive? Surely it was in order to see the day when our Lord, Christ himself, would make his final pilgrimage to Jerusalem, singing this psalm amongst others.

Jesus wept over the city which was to be destroyed within a generation. He forecast even more troubled times ahead, but also said 'When these (disasters) begin to take place, stand and lift up your heads, because your redemption is drawing near.' In the midst of mockery, defeat and despair, it is still true that

Luke 21:28

> *'Our help is in the name of the Lord,*
> *The Maker of heaven and earth' (v. 8).*

SURVIVAL

READING PSALM 125
'As the mountains surround Jerusalem, so the Lord surrounds his people both now and for evermore. The sceptre of the wicked will not remain over the land allotted to the righteous' (v. 2, NIV).

The historical circumstances of this psalm are obscure. The people of Israel were either in captivity, or being strongly persecuted. 'The sceptre of the wicked' was over their land. At such times it is easy to fear that everything you cherish is on the verge of extinction. There are places in today's world which suffer in the same way; where the church fights an uphill battle, where it seems 'the sceptre of the wicked' holds sway.

A new law in one African country prohibits religious meetings 'except in approved buildings' – the thin end of a wedge of persecution. In some countries there have been all-out campaigns to destroy the church, yet churches in those countries are full! In other areas campaigns to eradicate the church seem almost to have succeeded. In Iran there is a tiny, struggling church which needs our prayerful and practical support. Their Bishop, Dehqani Tafti, writes 'Our tiny church has to live under (persecution's) smoke and fire. This they are doing, gallantly, with a deep trust in the final victory of truth, no matter how weak it seems now'.

Christian Week, January 8th, 1988

Leonard Griffith writes on this theme 'Time and again the church has seemed doomed to extinction, yet the amazing thing is that always a miracle has happened, as though an invisible hand interposed to drive off the monster, push back the floodwaters and release the deadly trap.' In Saudi Arabia and certain other Muslim countries today the voice of the church is not just muted, but almost non-existent. But circumstances will change. We do believe that 'Those who trust in the Lord are like Mount Zion, which cannot be shaken'.

v. 1

'The story of the church is one of many resurrections.'
(John Calvin)

TO PONDER

THURSDAY 2 MARCH
A NEW BEGINNING

READING PSALM 126
'He who goes out weeping, carrying seed to sow, will return with songs of joy, carrying sheaves with him' (v. 6, NIV).

When, in 538 BC, Cyrus allowed many Jews to return to Judah after a couple of generations captivity in Babylon, they had great hopes of a new era of prosperity. They felt the Lord had done great things for them; that they were favoured above the rest of the nations (though Cyrus allowed some other captive nations, too, to return to their homelands); and everything would now be joy and laughter, praise and rejoicing. How soon their song changed! It was not easy to reap a harvest in their new land. For nearly twenty years the returned exiles suffered great hardship, sowing much and reaping little. Psalm 126 probably dates from that time.

Hag. 1:6

Vv. 1–3 reflect the excited hope of the first return from exile.
Vv. 4–6 reflect hardships the returned exiles faced.

In temperate, northern latitudes it is the season for sowing rather than reaping, but in many places it is harvest time. Many will rejoice as harvest is gathered in. Others, sadly, will be looking at their little crop, wondering if the effort was worthwhile. Over the years, we have seen the very climate change. Men tell us it is due to deforestation; to over-grazing; to inadequate methods of agriculture. There is much work to be done, not just sowing seed, but sowing thoughts, changing attitudes so that fortunes may be restored, and streams may once again flow. We need trees etc. to stop erosion. It is within man's power. May he use it. May those who today go out weeping with seed to sow, in future return with songs of joy, carrying sheaves with them.

Go then, though with weeping, sowing for the master,
Though the loss sustained our spirit often grieves
When our labour's over, he will bid us welcome;
We shall come rejoicing, bringing in the sheaves
(Knowles Shaw)

POPULATION EXPLOSION

READING PSALM 127
'Unless the Lord builds the house, its builders labour in vain. Unless the Lord watches over the city, the watchman stand guard in vain . . . Sons are a heritage from the Lord, children a reward from him' (vv. 1,3, NIV).

A: Anything done without God is pointless. B: The gift of many children is one of the greatest gifts given by the Lord. Conditions change. A: remains eternally true. B: raises very large questions. *(v. 1 — vv. 3–5)*

Good medical care can ensure survival of the vast majority of children into adulthood. Even in poor areas, longer life expectancy has caused a population explosion so fierce that world population will have increased tenfold in this century! Such increase cannot be sustained. Planning is needed or disaster will follow. Such ideas are unpopular in areas where children are desperately needed to provide for parents in their old age. They are even less popular where governments, indeed whole populations, see attempts to reduce population growth as a plot by rich nations to limit the influence of poor ones by reducing their numbers.

I remember the pride felt in Nigeria when population reached 50 million. Or again, try telling Kenyans their country cannot support more than 20 million. They rightly say, 'Britain has 50 million in less than half Kenya's area!' We can talk of climate, soils, different resources and other factors, but that is useless until the balance of society is changed, diverting resources from those who have to those who have not. This goes completely against economic principles which govern prosperous western democracies and eastern socialist states alike. Can such change occur? Indeed it can, but only when God's people take Psalm 127, v. 1 seriously.

Lord, we pray for trust between nations, particularly between those who claim to be friendly to each other, so that each may work with the other to make the most of the bounteous resources you have provided.   PRAYER

A VAIN PRAYER?

READING PSALM 128
'May you live to see your children's children. Peace be upon Israel'
(v. 6, NIV).

Until this century, life expectancy seems to have remained roughly constant. Some people have always reached old age, but more have died on the way there. In some societies today, with proper sanitation, clean water, vaccination against killer diseases and, more recently, antibiotics, the vast majority reach old age. It is a unique situation, unheard of before.

Until this century man was powerless to make the hope in Psalm 128 v. 6 a reality. Polluted water, unseen infection, ignorance about how disease spread, and many other factors worked against most people reaching old age.

Societies where the vast majority reach old age are still a tiny minority compared to world population. We have knowledge which could ensure long life for the vast majority. We do not have the political will to bring that knowledge to disadvantaged areas of the world, nor do we have the economic structures to allow such knowledge to be applied.

Psalm 128 provides a first step in bringing about prosperity for all. It stresses that a strong, supportive family structure is important. When the love, strength and support found within God-fearing, close, yet tolerant families reaches out into the wider community, from community to community and then from nation to nation; then it may be possible to re-structure economies; then it may be possible to spread knowledge around the world. Then it will be possible for you all to 'eat the fruit of your

v. 2   labour; blessings and prosperity will be yours.'

PRAYER   *Lord, hasten that day when all will share in the blessings enjoyed by a minority today. Help us to play our part by sharing our own blessings with family, friends and enemies alike. Amen.*

A FIERCE PSALM

READING PSALM 129
'May all who hate Zion be turned back in shame. May they be like grass on the roof, which withers before it can grow' (vv. 5,6, NIV).

Psalm 129 is not the fiercest in the book by any means. 58, 109 and, most of all 137 are even fiercer than this. But we cannot get away from the fact that Psalm 129 speaks of revenge, and pleads for the destruction of Zion's enemies. The revenge is not, however, a personal one. It seeks to maintain the integrity of Jerusalem, keeping it safe from invaders. Read Isaiah 10:28–32 to see the kind of attack Jerusalem faced throughout its history. That invasion, by Sennacherib, did not succeed. Later invasions did. Jesus, if he sang this psalm on his approach to Jerusalem, sang it knowing the city had been conquered, not just once but several times.

He knew, too, it would be conquered again. He wept over the fate about to fall on the city he loved *(Luke 19:41)*. He predicted its downfall after the disciples commented on the beauty of the temple *(Luke 21:5,6)*. He was in surroundings of conflict. As he sang this psalm he must have longed for the destruction of God's enemies. But that did not prevent him going through with the sacrifice demanded of him. He knew of his own coming 'destruction'.

Erik Routley comments on vv. 3,6,

'The ploughers must plough along his back, and make long furrows; also he must be as the dried grass along the housetops; he shall be taken away and there will be nobody to say "We bless you in the name of the Lord." On Palm Sunday, perhaps; but not on Good Friday. Then, only a shivering figure who at half past one in the morning curses and swears when a servant-girl mentions the name of Jesus. Our Lord's answer to this psalm of imprecation is to take upon himself both sides of the bloody fight. Thus, once again we have reconciliation.'

PRAYER SUBJECT: *Reconciliation.*
TO PONDER: *There is nothing easy about reconciliation. It involved the very 'destruction' of the Son of God himself.*

A TERRIFYING FORGIVENESS

READING PSALM 130
'If you, O Lord, kept a record of sins, O Lord, who could stand? But with you there is forgiveness; therefore you are feared . . . My soul waits for the Lord more than watchmen wait for the morning' (vv. 3,4,6, NIV).

What riches this psalm contains! From the fierce, destructive hope of Psalm 129, we enter suddenly into an atmosphere which breathes the New Testament attitude of forgiveness. Sometimes we cannot live with guilt, despite the assurance of forgiveness. The psalmist knew that, and he carefully maintains the awesome splendour of God. The forgiveness of God is not an easy forgiveness. Forgiveness is so hard that in order to be effective it demands the kind of sacrifice that Christ himself made.

The psalmist did not know Christ, but he understood how great, how wide, how fearsome God's forgiveness is.

Can it be true, did God's own son
Offer the gift supreme for me?
How can I pay so strong a debt,
Although I know the gift is free?

It breaks my heart, and bends my will,
It shatters my illusions vain,
It lets me hope for mercy still.
Fierce peace is mine amidst the pain.

And as I watch, throughout the night
Of this world's deep distress and fear,
I wait to see the heavenly light.
Praise God! Forgiveness does appear.

TO THINK
ABOUT

v. 4

With God there is forgiveness. God's forgiving love precedes people's repentance. It is his loving offer of forgiveness that moves them to repent.

READING PSALM 131
'My heart is not proud, O Lord, my eyes are not haughty . . . But I have stilled and quietened my soul, like a weaned child with its mother' (vv. 1,2, NIV).

This short psalm gives a delightful picture of peace in the Lord. Not very long ago, a TV evangelist's media sales director was trying to persuade the BBC to run his particular evangelist's programme. He said to the BBC man, 'The most important thing in the world is the preaching of the Lord Jesus Christ, and I would not like to be the person who has to account for hindering the spread of the Word, or obstructing truth. I don't know how such a person can sleep easy in his bed at night, for he will have to be accountable to the Lord for all the souls that have missed their chance to hear the saving news.'

His argument was a persuasive one. There is, of course, an element of truth in it. Every Christian has a responsibility to preach the Gospel. But how dangerous an argument it is! It is saturated with the presumptuous spirit which puts responsibility for the world onto our shoulders, instead of onto God's. Psalm 131 corrects that spirit.

Instead of anxiously scurrying from place to place, frantically persuading his readers that the salvation of the world depends on taking some particular course of action, our psalmist takes his rest in the Lord. He leans on him like a 'weaned child with its mother.' The weaned child no longer pulls frantically at his mother's breast, but instead rests and enjoys the warmth and comfort of his mother. Even so we can remain confident in God.

The psalms recognise that there is a time to raise urgent A THOUGHT
requests to God, and a time to wait on his will. Psalm 131
would have men work positively upon themselves, re-
straining their ambitions and desires with a godly
realism, calming themselves to contentment in God's
will.

(J. H. Eaton).

DAVID'S VOW

READING PSALM 132

'I will allow no sleep to my eyes, no slumber to my eyelids, till I find a place for the Lord, a dwelling place for the Mighty One of Jacob' (vv. 4,5, NIV).

1 Chr. 28:3

2 Chr. 3

David's vow, as recorded here, is not found in the history books which are left to us. Indeed, David was told that because of his warlike actions, it was not appropriate for him to build a temple for the Lord. He had to be content with erecting an altar on the threshing-floor of Araunah which became the site of Solomon's temple.

But though David was not allowed to build, in a real sense he found a dwelling place for the Lord in his own heart. His warrior past never really left him, yet we see his sensitivity to the workings of the Lord in his lament over Jonathan, in his treatment of Saul's other son, Ishbosheth, and above all in Psalm 51 'For I know my transgressions, and my sin is always before me . . . Create in me a pure heart, O God, and renew a right spirit within me.'

Jer. 33:31

Neither Solomon's temple, nor the second temple built by Haggai and Zechariah, but a third edifice, created by Herod, stood on Mount Zion as Jesus approached Jerusalem. The building was different. The people were different, but the worship was the same. Every year crowds came to celebrate the covenant God made, first of all with Abraham, then Moses, David and his successors. Jeremiah had once, long ago, revitalised temple worship with the promise of a New Covenant but only now, with Jesus approaching close to Jerusalem, taking part in that self-same process of worship that had gone on for centuries, was the New Covenant going to be realised. The descendant to be placed on David's throne is none other than our Lord, Jesus Christ himself.

TO PONDER   *Jesus' power is of a different order. The authorities of this world have usurped that power. Some have used military might and political force while claiming to act in the name of their Servant Lord. But always, ultimately, the powerless, sacrificial Servant conquers.*

READING PSALM 133
'How good and pleasant it is when brothers live together in unity'
(v. 1, NIV).

Pilgrimage to Jerusalem was a sign of unity, not just among brothers in a close-knit family, but of brotherhood between every Jew going to worship at the great feasts. The pilgrimages were times of national solidarity and family togetherness. Such unity is blessed. It is rare, so rare that it can be compared to the refreshing dews of Mt. Hermon falling on the sunbaked, dusty slopes of Zion. Hermon is cool, and snow-covered, the highest mountain in the Lebanon range. Zion is hot and busy, thronged with people who need cooling and refreshment.

Mt. Hermon also has another association. Some believe it was on Hermon that Christ was transfigured. That is the kind of experience we need if unity is to invade the communities of our modern world. The transfigured Christ must come like the refreshing dews of Mt. Hermon, to take the heat out of situations of terrible conflict. Ironically, nowhere on earth is that needed more in these days than on those very mountains, Hermon and Zion.

This tiny psalm which contains so much, ends with the clearest affirmation in the Old Testament that the Lord bestows the blessing of eternal life – an insight given to this psalmist long centuries before it became the accepted doctrine of Judaism and Judaism's most active offspring, the Christian Church.

A PRAYER*

Gracious Lord, who is not the God of discord or confusion, but the God of concord and of peace: join our hearts and affections together, so that we may walk as brothers in your house, in brotherly charity and love, and as members of the body of Christ. Let the oil of holiness, your Holy Spirit inflame us so that we may obtain life eternal through the same Jesus Christ.

*Prayer following Psalm 133, translated from the 1595 edition of the Scottish Metrical Psalter

THE QUESTION OF AUTHORITY

READING LUKE 20:1–8
'"Tell us by what authority you are doing these things," they said. "Who gave you this authority?"' (v. 2, NIV).

Today we begin reading Luke's account of Jesus' last few days of ministry in Jerusalem. We shall leave study of the entry into Jerusalem, along with the final Psalm of Ascent, till Palm Sunday.

The impression Luke gives of the first encounter with the authorities after cleansing the Temple, is that Jesus was trying to dodge a difficult situation, asking a second question in order to draw attention away from the one being asked. It's a familiar trick of politicians and others in authority.

Look more closely and we realise that Jesus' question gets to the heart of the matter. Jesus' authority came directly from God, but it also derived in a special sense from John. By allowing John to baptise him, he had associated himself with a reform movement within the Old Testament Jewish faith. Unless his questioners recognised that, and already accepted John's God-given reformation; unless they accepted the need for personal repentance, it was unlikely they would understand anything about Jesus' own authority.

Mark 1:15

Mark 1:27

Jesus' own first message had been 'repent and believe.' Early on in his ministry he had shown his authority. By making them cast their minds back to John, Jesus is continuing to make the same claims at the end of his ministry.

A THOUGHT   *Christians are all under authority, or as Dean Inge said, 'Christianity promises to make men free; it never promises to make them independent.'*

GOD SEEKS

READING LUKE 20:9–13
'Then the owner of the vineyard said, "What shall I do? I will send my son, whom I love, perhaps they will respect him"' (v. 13, NIV).

The Jewish scholar C. G. Montefiore once pointed out the main difference between Judaism and Christianity, as he saw it, by saying 'The Rabbis had said that if the sinner returns to God, God will receive him: they had not said that the love of God goes out to seek the sinner where he is. But in the Gospels it is so.'

Such statements are over-simplified, but this one highlights an important point in the controversy between Jesus and the authorities. It would be easy to dwell on the final part of today's story, and say that judgment will fall on the tenants, but there is a striking lesson to be learnt before that. Even the story of the lost son does not go so far as this story. The son had already decided to go back *Luke 15:20* to his father before the waiting father saw him far off and came to meet him. In today's parable (or allegory if you want to be more precise) there is a succession of messengers, each coming from the owner (God), each seeking what rightly belongs to the owner.

This idea of a seeking God is hard for us to accept. Most people seem to want to go out and find God. A lot of Christian terminology reinforces that idea. We talk, rightly, of Christianity as 'The Way'. We emphasise Jesus' words 'Seek and you shall find,' and that is good and proper. But we must not forget that God seeks us, too.

In The Salvation Army a simple chorus is often sung   BY THE WAY
    Meet my need, Lord; Meet my need, Lord;
        Meet my need, just now.
    I am waiting, and thou art coming,
        To meet my need just now.

*Note particularly line three: **I** am waiting, and **thou** art coming. Resist the temptation to change the order!*

GOD GIVES

READING LUKE 20:14–19
'What then will the owner of the vineyard do to them? He will come and kill those tenants and give the vineyard to others' (vv. 15b,16, NIV).

Never forget that awesome judgment fell on the tenants who rejected the vineyard owner's appeal. All who purposely reject and defy God will perish. Jesus was never afraid to warn men of the risk they ran. His strongest warnings were to the moral and religious leaders of the people. *(Matthew 16:1–4; Matthew 23:29–39)* Jesus was a Jew, so those he condemned most strongly were the Jewish leaders. Jewish leaders, then as now, were neither better nor worse than the vast majority of today's leaders, be they nominally Christian, Jew, Hindu, Muslim, Buddhist, adherents of any other religion, or of none.

The leaders of the people are the tenants of God's vineyard. When they do not fulfil their responsibilities the vineyard is given to others – given, says the NIV, not just rented. The rich, the powerful, the morally strong may be tenants. It is to the poor and down-trodden, the dependent and the under-privileged that God's gift is *given*. Today's society praises 'incentive' and 'reward' for effort, but God's rewards are not given according to merit. They are given by God's grace.

Human logic: Able men need high salaries to encourage them to give of their best to society.

God's logic: All men must practise self-sacrifice and humility. They cannot be judged by 'worth'. God, indeed, gives his vineyard to others.

PRAYER SUBJECT: *Christian stewardship.*

PRAYER: *Help us, Lord, to accept from your hand the gifts you give to us. Enable us to return to you what is your due. May we never feel that we 'deserve' the blessings we receive.*

RENDER UNTO GOD

READING LUKE 20:20–26
' "Whose image and superscription hath it?" They answered and said, "Caesar's." And he said unto them "Render therefore unto Caesar the things which be Caesar's, and unto God the things which be God's" ' (vv. 24,25, AV).

Many English speakers still have a strong, sometimes even sentimental attachment to the Authorised Version. Its ancient phrases; its 'Thee' and 'Thou'; its rolling succession of 'Ands' (12 in these seven short verses), give it a majestic ring that few other translations can match. Sometimes the word used in *AV* gives a more faithful rendering than its modern equivalents.

v. 24 'Render' is a good example. Few, if any, modern translations use this word, yet it is an almost exact translation of Luke's Greek. *didomi* means 'give.' The word Luke uses here, *apo – didomi*, means 'give back.' So render is exactly right.

By paying tax we are not just giving. We are giving *back* what is due. In return for the provision of conditions in which we can earn our daily living, we contribute to the common good. Few people enjoy doing this. Immediately we start to become prosperous we feel it is our right to hold on to what we have, instead of being willing to plough back resources into the very community that has made our gain possible. We want to control what we give, and reserve it for the causes we are interested in. Giving *back* to Caesar, in other words paying tax, means that we also have to give to less popular causes.

Government officials who are responsible for deciding how community resources are to be spent.

SUBJECT
FOR
PRAYER

TRICK QUESTIONS (I)

READING LUKE 20:27–38
'They can no longer die; for they are like the angels. They are God's children, since they are children of the resurrection' (v. 36, NIV).

Trick questions were meat and drink to Jesus. I get the feeling he enjoyed these awkward discussions with the experts, not just because he always won, for on one very unusual occasion he was actually upstaged by a woman, and it didn't seem to bother him! Rather he took delight in the exercise of his, and others' mental powers. Usually he answered a trick question with another question. But on this occasion his answer was direct.

Mark 7:28

Luke 20:24

John Stott writes 'Jesus began and ended his reply with a clear statement of their error. "You are wrong" he said (v. 24) "You are quite wrong" (v. 27). I confess that I find his outspokenness very refreshing.' He then adds

The Pharisees might well have been made uncomfortable by the Sadducees' question, for the Pharisees' notion of the next life was extremely materialistic. For example, 'the earth will assuredly restore the dead, which it now receives in order to preserve them, making no change in their form, but as it has received, so will it restore them.' (Apocalypse of Baruch 49:2) Hence posing resurrection riddles was a favourite game of the Sadducees and often an embarrassment to the Pharisees. But such questions would not embarrass Jesus, since he knew that the resurrection life would, by the power of God, be entirely different. 'When they rise from the dead,' he said, 'men and women do not marry; they are like the angels in heaven.'

1 Cor.
15:45–54

Here we see the basis for Paul's doctrine which we looked at earlier.

A THOUGHT   *The new age will be peopled by new beings living a new life under new conditions.*

(John Stott)

READING LUKE 20:39–44
'No one dared to ask him any more questions. Then Jesus said to them, "How is it that they say the Christ is the son of David?" ' (vv. 40,41, NIV).

Trick questions were not just asked by the Pharisees, Sadducees and others who wanted to embarrass Jesus. Sometimes Jesus asked trick questions himself. Today's reading contains a good example. It is a question hard to understand in today's youth-oriented culture. So little respect is paid to age. We tend to assume the young may one day be able to do things better. In Jesus' day the assumption was that things were always handled much better in the past.

People had a duty of reverence towards the older generation in a way quite foreign to today's world. The idea that a son could be greater than his father was unthinkable. The idea that an ancestor would ever address a descendant with deference seemed absurd. So when Jesus asks, 'How is it that they say the Christ is the son of David? . . . David calls him "Lord." How then can he be his son?' Jesus is at one and the same time setting out a real difficulty and asking a trick question. The only way of resolving the dilemma is to take it out of this world altogether.

If David calls the Christ, 'Lord' then he acknowledges that the Christ is not only human, but more than human. King David would not be able to call any human descendant of his, 'Lord' – but a heavenly descendant, that's another matter. It is in such simple ways that Luke puts forward the true nature of Christ. He is not just human, but also divine.

Doctrine in the Gospels is almost invariably taught by A THOUGHT
means of stories. Either stories told by Jesus, or stories told about Jesus.

THE GOSPEL OF THE 'HAVE-NOTS'

READING LUKE 20:45–21:4

'All these people gave their gifts out of their wealth; but she out of her poverty put in all that she had to live on' (v. 4, NIV).

'I'm all right Jack!' (implying it doesn't matter how you are), is the most unChristian phrase I can think of. Over and over again the message of Jesus comes through. Those who think they're all right are mistaken. As soon as we think we are all right, we stop being receptive to new ideas. We cease to be willing to listen properly to God.

Over and over again this contrast comes out in Luke's Gospel, the contrast between those who have and those who have not; the contrast between those who listen and those who do not; the contrast between those who will receive the Word and those who will not.

Luke 1:38; 1:18

Mary, the poor teenager waiting for her first child, listens. The priest Zechariah, doubts.

Luke 7:36–50

Simon the Pharisee is seen in contrast to the woman who is a sinner.

Luke 15:11–32

The virtuous son is contrasted with the prodigal.

Luke 14:23,24

The invited guests at the great supper are rejected, and the uninvited accepted.

Luke 18:15

The publican is justified, rather than the Pharisee.

Luke 18:15–17 compared to 18:18–30

Little children with nothing to give are contrasted with the rich and powerful ruler.

Look for other examples of such contrasts as you read Luke's gospel.

A PRAYER

Lord, you know how difficult it is for some of us to receive what you offer to us. You know how it is even harder to give away what we feel rightly belongs to us. Help us to follow the example of the poor widow, who received your Word and gave everything. Help us to identify with the poor and under-privileged. Guard us from pride and selfishness.

WHEN FACED BY DANGER

READING LUKE 21:5–28 (especially vv. 20–28)
'When these things begin to take place, stand up and lift up your heads, because your redemption is drawing near' (v. 28, NIV).

When faced by danger the natural tendency is to duck. Some animals even freeze and play 'dead'. On holiday in Norfolk we saw a frog, floating on the surface, all one-sided and apparently lifeless. I had accidentally touched it with a stick trailing in the water. We watched a long time, sorry the frog had been killed by such a little accident. Suddenly, when he felt the danger was over, he kicked and zoomed away into the depths. In a game park in Kenya we saw a dead jackal cub by the roadside, apparently run down by a passing car. Again we stopped. Again, when the danger seemed to be over, mother jackal came along and the 'dead' baby exploded into life, and trotted off after mum.

Faced by danger, Jesus' advice is exactly the opposite. Even the advice to flee, involves risk, actually being seen by the enemy running away. When danger threatens we need to stand up and be counted. It goes against every instinct of self-preservation. It is folly by any worldly standard, in the face of the dangers talked about in this chapter ranging from invasion by a ruthless enemy to vast, cosmic dangers which herald the coming End.   v. 21   v. 20   v. 26

Persecution leads to opportunities for witness. In all such conditions we have the support and the power of God with us.

> *Oft in danger, oft in woe,*
> *Onward, Christian, onward go:*
> *Let not fears your cause impede,*
> *Great your strength if great your need.*
> *(H. K. White and F. Fuller-Maitland, alt)*

This chapter does not tell us when the end will be, but gives strength to face the end whenever it comes.   A THOUGHT

NOT KNOWING

READING LUKE 21:29–38
'He told them this parable: "Look at the fig-tree and all the trees. When they sprout leaves, you can see for yourselves and know that summer is near. Even so, when you see these things happening you know that the kingdom of God is near"' (vv. 29–31, NIV).

Not knowing makes us feel uncomfortable. We prefer to know the worst, rather than be left hanging on without knowing. After a long period of being posted 'missing', it may even come as a relief to anxious relatives to know the worst fate of a loved one. The earlier faint hope that all may be well can sometimes be outweighed by the dreadful anxiety of not knowing.

We expect 'experts' to know. After years of teaching, and now writing comments on Scripture, people expect answers. When I seem uncertain, they write and tell me! Few are satisfied with a 'maybe' or a 'perhaps'. Yet even in Mathematics, which I, as a layman, think of as being very precise, some of the greatest advances seem to have occurred in areas where uncertainty can be accepted, and brought into the equation.

Jesus tells us we can know when the kingdom of God is near. The disasters already outlined are small-scale anticipations of the tremendous, awesome events which will occur. But disasters have shaken the world throughout history. In what sense, then, is the kingdom near? In the same sense as when Jesus started preaching. For all Mark 1:15 who will listen and repent the kingdom is at hand. For those who do not, the kingdom will break in upon them when they least expect it. The **final** consummation of the Kingdom – when that will be, none of us knows.

PRAYER *Eternal Father, who alone knows the final outcome of events, take away from us all tension related to ignorance. Give us strength to cope with the demands placed upon us even though we do not know the final outcome. Take away from us all unhealthy curiosity, yet keep our minds and hearts alert to the things which you have given us to know and to discover.*

READING PSALM 134, LUKE 19:41–46
'May the Lord, the maker of heaven and earth bless you from Zion'
(Psalm 134:3, NIV).
'It is written "My house will be a house of prayer"' (Luke 19:46, NIV).

Today we celebrate Jesus' arrival in Jerusalem. The final Psalm of Ascents which we read today reflects the psalmist's sheer delight and joy at the opportunity to go into the house of the Lord, 'the maker of heaven and earth.' As we read it and re-read it may we absorb its atmosphere and let its joy course through our hearts and spill over into today's celebration wherever we have opportunity to worship. At home, church, hall, or under the open sky.

It was a time of triumph, yet Luke brings out very clearly the pathos behind the celebration. As Jesus approaches, surrounded by cheering crowds, he weeps over the fate which is to befall the city. He throws the money changers out of the Temple, quotes an Old Testament verse, *(Isaiah 56:7)* and bemoans the fact that God's house of prayer has been turned into a den of thieves.

Note what Luke leaves out of the quotation. For a gospel written with gentiles in mind, it seems strange he omitted the words 'for all nations,' which are there in Mark. But Luke realised it was the temple of the old dispensation that Isaiah was talking about. Luke saw that as being exclusively Jewish. For Luke it is the Christian Church, rather than the Temple of the old dispensation, which is the vehicle for all nations to come to God.

> *Ride on, ride on in majesty!*
> *In lowly pomp ride on to die*
> *Bow thy meek head to mortal pain*
> *Then take, O God, thy power, and reign.*
> *(Henry Hart Milman)*

PRAYER SUBJECT: *Journeying with Jesus.*

PRAYER: *Take us with you, Lord, on your journey. We join your celebration in fulness of praise, but also feel your sorrow over those who do not know the things that belong to their peace (see v. 42).*

RETURN TO THE KINGDOM

READING LUKE 22:7–19
' "I tell you, I will not eat it again until it finds fulfilment in the kingdom of God" . . . And he took bread, gave thanks and broke it, and gave it to them, saying "This is my body given for you; do this in remembrance of me" ' (vv. 16,19, NIV).

Today we look again at the difficult concept of the kingdom of God. Jesus has told his disciples it is just round the corner, but no-one knows exactly when it will come. Now he is saying he won't eat or drink again until the kingdom has come.

Phil. 3:20   In a real sense the kingdom arrived with the death and resurrection of Christ. Every Christian is a citizen of the Kingdom of Heaven, not just a citizen of some future kingdom, but of one which now exists here in the Church, and in the hearts and lives of individual Christians. That kingdom was brought in by the submissive death of Jesus. That kingdom is one we all have the opportunity to be part of.

Being part of that kingdom involves sacrifice. Jesus says, 'This is my body given for you, do this in remembrance of me.' Every act of breaking bread reminds us of the sacrifice of Jesus. Salvationists witness to the fact that the sacrifice is paramount. Even formal remembrance by breaking bread can sometimes overshadow the real intention, which is that Christians should participate fully in Jesus' sacrifice.

'Do this in remembrance of me' involves sharing in the breaking of Jesus' body; being prepared to make the sacrifice he makes. When we forget that we exclude ourselves from the kingdom.

> Dear Saviour, I can ne'er repay
> The debt of love I owe.
> Here, Lord, I give myself away,
> 'Tis all that I can do.

(Isaac Watts)

READING LUKE 22:1–7; 20–23; 47–53
'Then Satan entered Judas, called Iscariot, one of the Twelve' (v. 3, NIV).
'The hand of him who is going to betray me is with mine on the table' (v. 21, NIV).
'Judas, are you betraying the Son of Man with a kiss?' (v. 48, NIV).

Why didn't Jesus do something? He knew he was going to be betrayed, yet still allowed it to happen. Jesus said 'woe to that man who betrays him' but as Leon Morris writes 'The phrase should not be taken in the sense of a curse: it is a lament. "Alas for that man" gives us the sense of it. We get the impression that the very way in which Jesus speaks of his betrayer constitutes an appeal to him even now to think again. The tenderness with which Jesus deals with Judas throughout this whole incident is very marked.'

Jesus knew his quarrel was not with Judas. Forcing Judas' mind would not alter the situation. Jesus was in conflict with the powers of darkness. Judas was, indeed, under the control of Satan, yet he was still responsible for his own actions. Jesus could not force him to change, any more than he could have yielded to Satan in the desert and still retained his integrity as Son of God.

Alec Vidler writes 'Free-will means the ability to choose between two alternatives, to choose what is good or what is bad. But freedom – Christian freedom – means being set free to choose spontaneously and without strain or conflict what is best.' Judas had been close to that freedom, as we are, too. We run the same risk as Judas. In spite of close contact with Christ, we may yet fail to choose what is best, if we are not in harmony with him.

'The grace of God does not compel us to choose what is best, but it enables us to do so freely and of our own accord.'

A QUOTE TO REMEMBER

(Alec Vidler)

ALL TWELVE

READING LUKE 22:24–38; 47–53
'The disciples said, "See, Lord, here are two swords." "That is enough," he replied' (v. 38, NIV).

Luke 9:46
Luke 9:19
v. 24

All twelve disciples deserted Jesus. All twelve left him to suffer alone. What sowed the seeds of that desertion? Misunderstanding. At the time of the transfiguration Peter, and the others, misunderstood its significance. In no time at all they were arguing about who would be greatest in the Kingdom. Prior to that they had not understood who Jesus really was. Even now they are puzzled. They are arguing at the supper table, still wanting the best places in the kingdom. You can be sure Peter would be involved!

Luke 10:4

compare
v. 51

After the argument Jesus spoke strong words, saying how Peter would deny him. Then the conversation turned to the use of force. The disciples had already argued about who would be greatest, and at this turn in the conversation it seems Jesus was becoming exasperated with their bickering. He tried to put a stop to it in his usual forceful way, with an ironic comment, 'If you don't have a sword, sell your cloak and buy one.' The disciples, oblivious to the bitter irony, unaware of the irrational contrast between their instructions at the start of the ministry and this sarcastic comment, now reply, 'See, here are two swords.' No wonder Jesus said 'It is enough.' A better translation might be 'No more of this!'

v. 51, John
18:10

Two swords against a posse of soldiers armed to the teeth! Indeed, when Peter used one of them, Jesus immediately healed the injured man. Violent rebellion has no place in the coming of the kingdom. Jesus suffers death instead.

A PRAYER

We take ourselves so seriously, Lord, that sometimes we don't know when you are gently mocking our misguided efforts. Make us sensitive to the tone of your voice as you speak to us, and guard us from over-reaction in all situations.

ONE DANGER OF PREJUDICE

READING LUKE 22:54–17
'In the middle of the courtyard . . . Peter sat down with them' (v. 55, NIV).
' "Certainly this fellow was with him, for he is a Galilean" ' (v. 59, NIV).

One danger of prejudice is that it is so easily confirmed. Just one or two instances where a prejudice proves to be justified and we can begin to think that particular prejudice is always justified. It was Passover time. Jews from all corners of the globe, and thousands from Galilee would be in Jerusalem for the feast. There was no need to suppose Peter was a follower of Jesus. It was the prejudice of the person who noticed his accent that made them say '**Certainly** he is one of them.' There was no certainty about it. But of course, Peter was one of them, not on account of his Galilean accent, but because he had been chosen by Our Lord himself.

In the mind of the person accusing Peter, all Galileans supported Jesus. Many British people think all Catholics in Ulster support the IRA. Some Irish citizens feel every Protestant in that same province supports the UDA. Neither prejudice is right. Yet it is right often enough, for the prejudice to be confirmed over and over again. This effect is heightened these days, for so many people whose actions are reported in the press or seen on TV are those about whom the prejudice is correct!

Fighting prejudice is not easy. It has a strength of its own. It feeds on itself. It is deepened by every occasion on which it is confirmed. It is rarely lessened by those occasions on which it is found to be false.

We can see prejudice in others. It is almost impossible to A THOUGHT
see in ourselves. That is the real danger.

AN UNHOLY ALLIANCE

READING LUKE 23:1–23
'That day Herod and Pilate became friends – before this they had been enemies' (v. 12, NIV).

Luke alone tells us that Pilate sent Jesus to Herod, ruler of Galilee, who was in Jerusalem for the Passover feast. Herod was jealous of Pilate. Herod wanted to be ruler of the whole of Palestine, not just Galilee. The Roman governor, Pilate, stood in his way.

Pilate knew about Herod's ambition. Sending Jesus to him achieved two things. It gave Pilate a chance to make Herod feel important, and thus friendly towards him. It gave Pilate a slim chance of avoiding responsibility for Jesus' death. He achieved the first, but not the second. Herod was not going to get caught a second time. He had ordered the death of John the Baptist after being tricked by his wife, Herodias. He was not going to risk ordering the death of Jesus.

Mark
6:17–27

However, he was still taken in by Pilate's scheming, and ironically, the trial of Jesus brought about friendship between sworn enemies. Or is it ironic? Surely that is the whole point of the death of Jesus. In a strange way it brings about reconciliation, friendship between enemies. We cannot explain it. We can only feel it.

George Bennard's emotional hymn captures this feeling. No explanation. Just a simple statement. But what power it has!

O that old rugged cross, so despised by the world,
Has a wondrous attraction for me;
For the dear Lamb of God left his glory above
To bear it to dark Calvary.

Christ's death on the Cross has made peace with God for all.

(Colossians 1:20, LB)

AN IN-BETWEEN DAY

READING LUKE 23:44–56
'The centurion . . . praised God and said, "Surely this was a righteous man." . . . But all those who knew him, including the women who had followed him from Galilee, stood at a distance. . . . Then they went home and prepared spices and perfumes' (vv. 47,49,56, NIV).

Today is an odd day, an in-between day, between the gruesome events of Good Friday and the unspeakable joy of Easter Day. It is, in the words of the Apostles' creed, the day when Jesus descended into hell. A dark day which used to be known as the Black Sabbath. It is particularly poignant this year. Today, 25 March, is the feast of the Annunciation. Today we remember the angel announcing to Mary that she was to be the mother of Jesus. How strange that Luke makes no mention of Mary's reaction at the cross. He gave us exquisite detail concerning the birth of Jesus; Mary's thoughts and feelings; the reaction of the relatives. But at the cross he makes no distinction between Mary and the other women who followed from Galilee. It is John who describes the conversation between Mary, Jesus and the other disciple. Possibly Luke felt it was intruding too much into private grief to relate the things that Mary said about the cross.

Luke 1:30–32

John 19:26,27

How did Mary feel? What did she think? Was she beginning to understand? Did the centurion's reaction remind her of the words the angel had spoken, thirty four years before? I like to think it did. At the moment the centurion exclaimed 'Surely this was a righteous man' and added, 'Surely he was the Son of God' Mary's heart would be moved, not just to sorrow, but to remembrance of all that had happened, and particularly of the angel's visit.

v. 47

Matt. 27:54

One of today's psalms in the Anglican liturgy is Psalm 131. Read those few short verses again. Can you enter in to Mary's thoughts and feelings?

This in-between day, do you look on it as a sad day or a happy one?

TO THINK ABOUT

RESURRECTION AND REHABILITATION

READING LUKE 24:1–12
'Peter, however, got up and ran to the tomb. Bending over, he saw the strips of linen lying by themselves, and he went away, wondering to himself what had happened' (v. 12, NIV).

Easter Sunday! What a glorious day! A day of rest and praise. Yet the first Easter Day was an ordinary working day. The Sabbath was over. All the hustle and bustle of the big city was starting again, and the thoughts of the disciples would be turning to work, and earning their living, now that Jesus had gone.

Peter felt dreadful about denying Jesus. Did any other disciple know how he felt? The gospels don't say. We can only imagine. Did Peter bottle his feelings up? Usually he was impetuous, wilful, only too ready to speak or shout out what was on his mind. But to admit to the others he had denied knowing Jesus – that I can't imagine even Peter doing at that stage. Think of his relief, then, when he could actually go and do something. Being an ordinary working day, he could RUN to the tomb. He was probably ready to attack the people who had disturbed it. Did he still have his sword from the garden incident just over 48 hours before? Would he have gone now to the very death, fighting for his Lord to make up for the denial? The questions are endless.

Peter was stopped short by the angel, telling him of the risen Lord. It took weeks more before Peter was finally restored. Not until Pentecost did he become powerful for God. But his rehabilitation started as he RAN to the tomb.

PRAYER SUBJECT: *Enthusiasm for the gospel.*
PRAYER: *On this glorious, holiday Easter Morning, thank you Lord, for Peter's change of direction. Thank you for the impetus which sent him running to the tomb. Change us, too, Lord. Make us as keen as Peter to run to you for strength and healing, and above all to share in your resurrection life.*

THE UNKNOWN CHRIST

READING LUKE 24:13–27
'As they talked and discussed these things with each other, Jesus himself came up and walked along with them . . . And beginning with Moses and all the Prophets, he explained to them what was said in all the Scriptures concerning himself' (vv. 15,27, NIV).

Luke does not let us forget how hard it is to realise exactly who Jesus is. Two disciples, not in the Twelve, but possibly a part of that larger band who went on the mission of the Seventy, were returning to their home in Emmaus. They were joined by the risen Lord, yet did not recognise him. Even the Twelve spent years with him without realising fully that Jesus' kingdom was not of this world. It is hardly surprising that these two were unable to recognise Jesus in his risen state.

Luke 10:1

We have an advantage over them. For two thousand years men have had the chance to recognise the risen Christ. Yet aren't we also often unaware that we have been with Jesus? We receive inspiration which we should attribute to our Lord, yet we try to find some other explanation. We rationalise it as emotion. We see it as the simple naivety of a child. We wonder at the skill of an artist, musician, or actor. Many people still have Emmaus Road experiences, when, despite a 'burning in the heart' they do not recognise the Christ who is walking with them. Arch Wiggins, expresses this in a personal way in a song based on this incident

I set out a pilgrim, sad at heart, to walk a lonely road
Doubt had marred my simple trusting, doubt a future ill
*   forebode*
And as I pondered o'er my grief, my shattered hope
*   and unbelief,*
A stranger, to my soul's relief, drew near and walked
*   with me.*
*   Jesus himself drew near, Jesus himself drew near*
*   When alone on the road, oppressed by my load*
*   Jesus himself drew near and walked with me.*

SOMETHING SPECIAL IN THE EVERYDAY

READING LUKE 24:28–35
'When he was at the table with them, he took bread, gave thanks, broke it and began to give it to them. Then their eyes were opened and they recognised him' (v. 30, NIV).

Even if you are hurrying to avoid nightfall, or robbers waiting for the unwary, a walk of seven miles doesn't just take a couple of minutes! Jesus spent a long time expounding the Scriptures to these two. He went through, from Moses onwards, talking all the time about himself. What a privilege, to hear it from the lips of our Lord! But they would never have known who he was, if they hadn't invited him in.

There's a lesson there, of course, a lesson of hospitality. When we give, how often we receive so much more in return. It is a valuable lesson, but even more remarkable is the way that insight dawned upon these two disciples. It came in the ordinary action of breaking bread. Now Cleopas and his friend had not been at the Last Supper. So they did not remember the highly charged, emotive action of that meal. Jesus' action was the ordinary, everyday action of breaking bread. Whenever he shared a meal, that ordinary action became special.

Christians today have the same opportunity. On numerous occasions when they break bread with others, Jesus may be seen and recognised. Not only on the 'soup runs' when salvationists and others break bread with the homeless in some of the great cities of the world, not just in the relief camps where Christian Aid and others bring much needed emergency aid – but also when we invite our next door neighbour, a school friend, a relative.

A PRAYER   *Remind us, Lord, as we eat in company with other people today, of your action in breaking bread. May the way that we approach our meal remind us of your action at Emmaus. May we use all the resources you give to us reverently, acknowledging their origin, and sharing them with others as Your gift to them.*

READING LUKE 24:33–44
'Jesus said to them "Peace be with you" . . . Why are you troubled, and why do doubts rise in your minds? Look at my hands and feet. It is I myself"' (vv. 36,38,39, NIV).

Luke wants to demonstrate very clearly the reality of Jesus' resurrection body. His hands and feet are still wounded. He eats in their presence. Yet at the same time he can, as at Emmaus, vanish from their midst. His presence is real, yet elusive.

Many scholars think the little phrase 'Peace be with you' was added to the text of Luke by a later hand. It is missing from many manuscripts, and is the same as the phrase at John 19:20. The answer as to whether it really belongs in Luke's text still eludes scholars. *NEB, RSV, LB* and others omit it.

But peace itself is an elusive quality. Jesus left his peace with us, yet like those disciples of old, many are still troubled, doubting and lacking in the serenity that Christ can give.

The very strength of efforts made to attain peace somehow tends to place it beyond our grasp. Imagine a donkey with a carrot dangling in front of him. The carrot hangs from a stick. The stick is fixed to the donkey's collar. However far he goes forward in order to reach the carrot, it is always beyond him. The poor donkey can never reach it. But when he has given up the struggle, become so weary that he lies down and accepts defeat, the string becomes slack as the carrot touches the ground, and our donkey can reach it.

The donkey in fact already has the carrot, but the only way he can enjoy its benefits is to give up striving for it!

'A great many people are trying to make peace, but that has already been done. God has not left it for us to do; all we have to do is to enter into it.' A THOUGHT ABOUT PEACE

(Dwight L. Moody)

WORK AND WORSHIP

READING LUKE 24:45–53
'Repentance and forgiveness of sins will be preached in his name to all nations, beginning at Jerusalem . . . He left them and was taken up into heaven. Then they worshipped him and returned to Jerusalem with great joy' (vv. 47,51,52, NIV).

Worship and work. Both are necessary. One without the other is either meaningless or ineffective.

This story of the Ascension of Jesus can easily be misunderstood. When we think of Jesus who has ascended into heaven the temptation is to wonder where he is, where heaven is, and where God is. We want to look for a physical presence. The Russian astronaut who said he had not seen God out there in space thought he had said something significant. But Christians would not expect to see the ascended Christ in space any more than we would expect to see him, physically, on earth.

Wherever Christians are and whenever they worship, there the ascended Christ is amongst them. It is significant that the disciples worshipped him after his ascension. They saw it happen, and for them 'ascension' was the right word. But for us it is not really adequate. As D. B. J. Campbell writes 'The ascension story is not meant to make known the actual location of heaven. Perhaps in the twentieth century, instead of calling the commemoration of this event Ascension Day, although it was that for the disciples, it would be better to say Exaltation Day. This would be a reminder that when we use our inadequate human language to speak of God and Christ as "up", "high", or "above", we use these terms not literally, but in the way in which we commonly do to denote priority, rank, position or authority.'

A PRAYER *Lord, we cannot see what those earliest disciples did. But we can share in their worship. We, too, can lift you up, Jesus, in our hearts. We can raise you to a position of authority in our lives. May our continued study of your Word enable us to give you the rightful place of complete priority in everything and over everything.*

IN A PAGAN SOCIETY
(The books of Ruth and Esther)

Two Old Testament books are named after women, and have women as the main characters. This makes them different from the rest – and continues our theme of diversity within the Scriptures.

Ruth has a historical setting. It supplies details of King David's ancestors, lacking in the books of Samuel where you might expect to find them. Esther is a romantic story of the origins of Purim, most recent of the great Jewish festivals, the only festival to originate after the Exile, i.e. after 520 BC. Ruth emphasises that even the most unlikely people are welcome in the Jewish community. Esther stresses the great difference between Jews and others. Esther is the only book in the Bible which has no mention of God.*

More heat than light is created by scholars discussing the date of these two books. Ruth's date is very uncertain. Either it was written close to the time of David, or else much later, about the time of Nehemiah. Esther came much later, probably in the period of Jewish victory, following long persecution by the Syrians in the first half of the second century BC.

The following table summarises the points above:

RUTH	ESTHER
Main character is a woman	Main character is a woman
Historical Romance	A tale of intrigue
Interest in non-Jews	Interest in Jews
Highlights origins of King David	Highlights origin of the feast Purim
	Does not mention God*
Date 950 BC or about 440 BC	Date 150 BC or so.

*Though in paraphrasing, LB does sometimes refer to God. (See 12 April.)

A DESPERATE SITUATION

READING RUTH 1:1–5
'In the days when the judges ruled there was a famine in the land, and a certain man of Bethlehem in Judah went to sojourn in the country of Moab' (v. 1, RSV).

Try to imagine, if there was famine today in Israel, a Jewish family fleeing to Jordan, or even Syria! Such a picture gives some idea of Elimelech's desperate situation. Judah and Moab were just as strong enemies then, as Israel and Jordan, or Israel and Syria are today.

When the book of Ruth was written its language was, even then, old-fashioned. Today's *RSV* quote tries to keep the ancient flavour through old-fashioned words, e.g. 'sojourn', and the old-fashioned expression 'a certain man of . . .' But that old, old story is always new. Famine is still with us. Refugees still flee from it. Others flee from political persecution, or simply to try and provide better lives for their families. They face not only the physical hardships of immigrant life, but also the emotional disturbance of life in unfamiliar surroundings, often among hostile people.

Hostility may be open. Anti-immigrant slogans can still be seen scrawled on walls in British cities, giving many the uncomfortable feeling of not being wanted. Sometimes hostility is less open, and perhaps harder to deal with. Successive job rejections with no real reason given, make it hard to believe that skin colour or immigrant status have nothing to do with it.

In spite of this, immigrants do still make new lives for themselves, and some even marry into the 'host' community. Elimelech's sons did just that. They grappled with the problems of life in two cultures. Remaining faithful to Yahweh but also relating to Moabite institutions would be like walking a tightrope over Niagara. Pray for today's immigrants; loyalty to their origins so often conflicts with easy relationships in the new community.

TO PONDER   *What positive steps am I taking to make life easier for strangers or immigrants within my community?*

READING RUTH 1:6–14
'Orpah kissed her mother-in-law goodbye, and returned to her child-hood home; but Ruth insisted on staying with Naomi' (v. 14, LB).

With husband and both sons dead, Naomi decided to return home. A single woman without land or family had no means of support. Once back home in Judah she could hope to be cared for by someone, some responsible relative. No one had responsibility for her in Moab. She was destitute. Such are the risks taken by immigrants, now as then. How important it is that countries should have humane and liberal immigration laws. How vital to allow for entry of dependents and family for, unfortunately, return doors are often shut upon today's immigrant. Naomi was better off in her day!

By Jewish law widows like Ruth and Orpah were supposed to marry a brother of their former husband. No brother survived. In that direction there was no hope, but both felt a moral obligation to their mother-in-law.

For Orpah the pull of family soon overcame her feeling of obligation. We cannot condemn her. She was in a dilemma. Whatever she did was likely to be wrong. Going with Naomi she risked destitution. Naomi's family might well reject her, a Moabitess. Her contact with Naomi and with Naomi's religion will have taught her that 'No Moabite will ever enter the sanctuary, even after the tenth generation'. On the other hand, back home she had no guarantee of a satisfactory marriage, even though less likely to be destitute.

Deut. 23:3

For Ruth the strong personal tie overcame everything. She took the risk.

No longer in bondage my freedom I'll use
My Master to serve in the way he shall choose;
To work or to witness, to go or remain,
His smile of approval my infinite gain
(Charles Coller)

EXTRAVAGANT LANGUAGE

READING RUTH 1:15–22

'Where you go I will go, and where you lodge I will lodge; your people shall be my people, and your God my God; where you die I will die, and there I will be buried. May the Lord do so to me and more also if even death parts me from you' (vv. 16–18, RSV).

Ruth's vow is more like a marriage vow than a pledge to a mother-in-law. Her love for Naomi, her sense of obligation is such, that she will not leave her. Today such devotion would be misunderstood. An ulterior motive would be assumed, or some unhealthy aspect in the relationship suspected. But for the author of this delightful book Ruth's motives are entirely pure. He (or she?) describes the strength, power, and beauty of this relationship so perfectly that even Goethe was driven to say that the story of Ruth was the most perfect story he knew.

But Naomi, at this stage, is unaware of Ruth's devotion. She doesn't hear what her daughter-in-law is saying. Like the possessed man who did not want to be free of the devils inside him (*Mark 5:10*). Naomi, too, wants to cling to her sorrow and emptiness. David Clines writes 'Naomi wishes her daughters-in-law back in Moab and out of her life, so that outwardly also her life may appear to be as empty as she feels it is inwardly. She has not noticed that Ruth is dedicating herself to her . . . she hears only the girl's determination, and knows no words for responding to her love.'

At this point of the story things could have gone tragically wrong. Few of us would have persevered like Ruth did. Just imagine the hurt when Naomi says '**I went away full, and the Lord has brought me back empty**.' Ruth's devotion, her support, her loyalty, her love were all ignored completely by Naomi. The risk was becoming even greater, yet still Ruth persevered.

PRAYER SUBJECT: *For carers.*

PRAYER: *Thank you, Lord, for those who are willing to care for others even when their care is not appreciated. May they be strengthened in their resolve to go on caring. May they know that you are with them in their task.*

EXTRAVAGANT ACTION

READING RUTH 2:1–7
'The foreman replied ... She went into the field and has worked steadily from morning until now, without resting even for a moment' (vv. 6,7, NIV).

The title of today's comment may cause some surprise, for surely working steadily is not remarkable enough to warrant the title 'extravagant action', or is it? The word extravagant is not just used to tie today's comment in with yesterday's – though admittedly the idea came from using the word yesterday. It is used because extravagant language is meaningless unless it is backed up by action. Ruth could have pledged loyalty for ever and ever, for as long as she liked, but without going and gleaning her words would be as empty as the resounding gong or clanging cymbal that Paul speaks about.   1 Cor. 13

Gleaning, like sojourn, is an old-fashioned word. It also refers to an old-fashioned idea. Today we try to extract every last ounce of productivity from the soil. Crop yields become greater and greater. The last thing in the mind of any farmer is to leave part of the crop for others to be able to glean. But that is exactly what the Jewish law required. It not only required that some of the   Lev. 19:9–10 crop should be left unharvested, but that it should be left for the 'sojourner'. That is to say, for the stranger, the   Lev. 19:10, RSV immigrant. Positive discrimination may be one of today's 'in' words, but it is also an Old Testament idea. The disadvantages suffered by immigrants require positive efforts on their behalf by the host community. In Germany many are called 'Gastarbeiter' – literally 'guest-workers'. O that they might be treated as guests, with politeness and care for their comfort, instead of being looked on as just another resource, exploitable like the land from which we wring every last ounce of productivity.

Do I treat my immigrant neighbour truly as a guest rather   TO PONDER *than an intruder? Can I go on from there to treat him truly as a brother?*

A BLEAK FUTURE

READING RUTH 2:8–23
'Ruth stayed close to the servant girls of Boaz to glean until the barley and wheat harvests were finished. And she lived with her mother-in-law' (v. 23, NIV).

April – May

Ruth and Naomi came to Bethlehem at the beginning of the barley harvest. While the harvest lasted, all was well. That harvest was now over. What then? Gleaning is fine in an emergency, but that is all. A long term strategy was needed. Ruth had worked to establish her reputation. Days of hard labour had lengthened into weeks and months. Boaz's generosity meant she and her mother-in-law would probably not have starved, but for a full life they needed more than just the gleanings from the rich man's field.

While Ruth was innocently working, Naomi was scheming. So far Ruth seems to have had the rough end of it. She works. Naomi profits. Life is like that.

From one point of view it is exploitation. Naomi is exploiting Ruth's devotion. Dreadfully capitalist! From another viewpoint we see in practice Karl Marx's dictum 'From each according to his ability, to each according to his need!' Naomi, physically weak but mentally able, makes the plans. Ruth carries them out. Appallingly Marxist! Whichever view you take the result is the same. Both benefit.

Whichever view you take, if either side fails to keep their part of the bargain, both suffer. As soon as mutual trust and confidence break down tragedy results. In the story of Ruth, trust remains. In today's society where can we find such trust? If not in ourselves, then where?

TO PONDER   *If I trust Jesus fully, will I not also trust my fellows?*

A PRAYER   *I trust you, Lord Jesus. Help me overcome my suspicion of others.*

NAOMI'S SCHEMING CONTINUES

READING RUTH 2:11, Chapter 3
'Boaz replied, "I've been told all about what you have done for your mother-in-law since the death of your husband' (2:11, NIV).
**'"This kindness is greater than that which you showed earlier . . . And now, my daughter, don't be afraid. I will do for you all you ask. All my fellow-townsmen know that you are a woman of noble character"'
(3:10, NIV).**

By any standard Naomi's behaviour is questionable. Her scheming puts Ruths' reputation at risk. In one way her actions are worse than those of the unjust steward in Jesus' parable. He at least only put his own reputation on the line. Naomi was compromising someone else. But a redeeming feature in this strange story is once more trust. This time both Ruth and Naomi trust and take a risk.

Luke 16:1–8

Ruth trusted Naomi, and risked her own reputation, for if Boaz made a fuss and threw her out she would be branded as a prostitute.

Naomi trusted Boaz. She believed Boaz was an upright man who would not want to damage Ruth's reputation. True, she risked Ruth's reputation rather than her own. But she also risked her own livelihood. If her estimate of Boaz had been wrong, he would not have married Ruth – and Naomi would not have been provided for!

*compare
Joseph,
Matt. 1:19*

How complex this simple story is! How carefully we need to read it in order to get at the message behind it, the message of trust in a devious world! We need to be 'shrewd as snakes' and a wee bit more.

Matt. 10:16

> *Oft our trust has known betrayal,*
> *Oft our hopes were vain,*
> *But there's One in every trial*
> *Constant will remain.*
>
> *Yesterday, today, for ever,*
> *Jesus is the same;*
> *We may change, but Jesus never;*
> *Glory to his name!*
> *(Richard Slater [verse] A. B. Simpson [chorus])*

REDEMPTION – AT A PRICE

READING RUTH 4:1–6
Kinsman: 'I will redeem it'
Boaz: 'On the day you buy the land . . . you acquire the dead
            man's widow in order to maintain the name of the dead
            with his property.'
Kinsman: 'Then I cannot redeem it because I might endanger my own
            estate'   (vv. 4b,5,6, NIV).

Boaz acted quickly. He did not want to be embarrassed by scandalous stories going around. Maybe he had grown genuinely fond of Ruth. Surely he didn't just see her as a useful asset, hardworking and loyal. Though even that possibly affected his actions.

According to the ancient custom, he offered Naomi's land to Elimelech's closest relative. Land? How wonderful! The relative was keen, and immediately said '**I will redeem it**.' How quickly his plans changed when he knew that with the land he had to take Ruth! That was different. Boaz probably had children of his own already. He had no worries about Ruth's children carrying the name of Elimelech. The closest kinsman did need to worry. He risked ruining his own inheritance. In this story all ends happily, for Boaz and Ruth are pleased the kinsman will not fulfil his obligation. But how different it could have been!

The ancient dilemmas look different today, against a different cultural background, but in essence they are the same. There are fewer societies today where buying the land involves taking the girl who goes with it, but we still need guidance to make the right decisions. We still have to face the consequences of those decisions, and trust that we will get the balance right between ourselves, others, and God.

TO PONDER *Redemption is costly. It involves risk. For some, to follow Christ means to reject family and friends. For some it means sacrificing an inheritance.*

For others it means accepting family obligations, and sacrificing wider ambitions.

FLAVOURS OF THE PAST

READING RUTH 4:7–12
'Now this was the custom in former times in Israel' (v. 7, RSV).

The custom of taking off a shoe and giving it to another as a sign that a contract has been made, had to be explained for the readers at the time when Ruth was written. The custom of levirate, also an old one, did not need explaining then, but does need explaining to most readers today. see 1 April

In this passage there are other echoes of the past; Rachel and Leah, and Tamar. By mentioning them the author is recognising again the potential dangers faced by – or possibly brought about through? – Ruth the Moabitess. Rachel and Leah sought from afar by Jacob had little love for each other and caused much domestic upheaval. The unsavoury incident of Tamar's relationship with Judah brought the house of Judah close to complete disaster and disrepute, not through Tamar's own fault, but as a result of Judah's failure to fulfil the requirements of the 'levirate' law.

Gen. 28

Gen. 38

Ruth's acceptance into the mainstream of life in Israel will not be easy for her. It will not be easy for Israel. Changing one's country, and one's loyalties is never easy. There are great potential dangers. But there can also be great rewards. Ruth accepted the challenge so fully that she became the ancestress, not only of David the great King of Israel, but of Christ himself.

How has the life of my own country been enriched by those who have come from other cultures in the past?   TO THINK ABOUT

Use this space to jot down a couple of examples.   USE THIS SPACE

THE IMMIGRANT'S LOT

READING RUTH 4:13–22
'Now at last Naomi has a son again' (v. 16, LB)

We hinted yesterday that things could not have been easy for Ruth. Read the whole story again today if you have time, especially if you have the *Living Bible* version available. Notice how, despite Ruth's name being retained in the title of the book, so much of it centres on Naomi.

1:20

It is Naomi who wishes to be renamed 'Mara' or bitterness, following her tragedy. It is Naomi who takes the initiative in going back to Judah. It is Naomi who intrigues to get Ruth married off; Naomi who nurses the child of the marriage, and Naomi to whom the women say 'She has a son again.' Poor Ruth, it is almost as though she didn't exist.

see comment
of Sunday 2

Ruth is hardly treated as a person in her own right for most of this story. She is pushed here and there. She is tolerated in Judah, but her part in giving Boaz an heir, and King David an ancestor, is ignored in the final genealogy. Even her husband – who should by right have featured in the final list of David's forebears at v. 22 – is pushed out in favour of Boaz.

Many today face similar frustrations. They give their lives and their loyalty to a host community, and receive little recognition. Decades, perhaps even centuries later, though, Ruth was remembered. She was remembered by the writer of this book we have studied. Later still Matthew in his gospel featured her in his genealogy of Jesus. Perhaps, one day, such recognition will be afforded to today's immigrants – but how much better if host communities could recognise quickly the positive contributions made by the guests in their midst, and act accordingly.

TO PONDER   *Honouring people at a distance is easy. How much harder to value them when they are right next to us.*

READING ESTHER 1
'"Queen Vashti has wronged not only the king but every official and citizen of your empire. For women everywhere will begin to disobey their husbands when they learn what Queen Vashti has done"' (vv. 16,17, LB).

Who insulted whom? The king who expected his queen to parade in front of a crowd of drunken oafs, or the queen who refused to be humiliated? How priggish and conceited men can become. How afraid of losing their power to women. Read this chapter carefully, especially v. 10 onwards. You will see not only the worst aspects of relationships in a society where women are not given the respect due to them, but also the worst aspects of relationships between any powerful group and those that they feel it is their right to control.

A British politician recently said that we had now got beyond the stage where workers thought firms were run for their benefit, back to the proper position where they knew firms were run to benefit shareholders. God help any worker who feels entitled to respect and decent working conditions when influential politicians feel like that! It is the same phenomenon we see here in Esther. One society thinks women are inferior, and must be kept in their place. Another thinks workers are inferior, and must be kept in theirs.

It's all done in the name of good order, the smooth working of society, or the natural scheme of things. If you had talked to the advisers of King Ahasuerus about human dignity, they wouldn't have understand you. Questioning a man's right to lord it over his wife was treason. In many societies today, questioning the right to 'profit' is looked on as almost treasonable. Question that assumption and you will hardly be understood. But such assumptions, e.g. assumptions of male superiority, the assumption of a 'right' to profit, the assumption that some people are 'superior', and many others – must be questioned if human dignity is to be preserved.

PRAYER SUBJECT: *For the respecting of human rights.*
PRAYER: *Make us sensitive, Lord, to the rights and needs of others. Help us not to look at people in economic terms, but to value every human being.*

ESTHER'S QUALITIES

READING ESTHER 2:1–8,15–23
'When it was Esther's turn to go to the king ... all the other girls exclaimed with delight when they saw her' (v. 15, LB).

Esther's qualities were good looks, obedience, modesty and charm. Among the girls brought before the king so he could choose a new queen to succeed brave Queen Vashti, Esther stood out. Some people are like that. However modest, retiring or self-effacing they try to be, they stand out in a crowd and something draws us to them. Such people, of course, are rare but they do exist – Mother Theresa for instance.

But among Esther's great qualities there is one most surprising one. How Esther managed to keep secret the fact that she was a Jewess, we shall never know.

We can argue till the end of time about historical details of the book of Esther. Was Ahasuerus simply another name for Xerxes, as the *Good News Bible* assumes? Is there any evidence outside the Old Testament that Xerxes (Ahasuerus) had a queen called Vashti, and a second queen called Esther? Is it possible that someone taken captive by Nebuchadnezzar could still be alive 120 years later? Different scholars give different answers to such questions. The evidence is slight, and in many cases conflicting. But one thing that could make me doubt whether Esther is historical is this detail. She kept her religion secret.

2:5

Without that secrecy, the story would lose its point. It is necessary to the plot, yet how could someone with Esther's qualities keep her Jewishness secret? It baffles me. It goes completely against the grain. It must have been an enormous sacrifice for Esther to keep quiet about her faith. Yet how often those who are free to witness shrink back from making that witness!

TO THINK
ABOUT
Do I find it hard to keep quiet about my beliefs? If not, is something wrong with my faith?

DIFFERENT? THEN DIE!

READING ESTHER 3
' "There is a certain race of people scattered through all the provinces of your kingdom," he began, "and their laws are different from those of any other nation . . . therefore it is not in the king's interests to let them live" ' (v. 8, LB).

What can explain how over and over again throughout history, Jews have been hounded and persecuted, insulted and reviled? Are they really that much worse than other people? The evidence would seem to state exactly the opposite. In many, many fields of human endeavour, in science, the arts, finance, medicine and, naturally, religion the achievements of Jews have been out of all proportion to their small numbers. Perhaps that ability to achieve great things has caused jealousy. Perhaps their sense of always being right infuriates others. But I would suggest that both their greatness and their persecution arise from the simple fact that they are different, and insist on maintaining that difference whatever the cost.

Difference, at a distance, may be entertaining. It is delightful to travel and see different sights, take in a different culture. Some travellers try to bring back some of the different ideas, different values they have come in contact with. That is fine, and may become quite fashionable – as witness the great upsurge of interest in eastern culture when some of the Beatles found a guru, way back in the sixties. But when groups of people within our own community turn out to be different, tensions arise. We have already looked at the difficulties immigrants face.

Does the simple fact of difference mean that tension and mistrust are inevitable? TO PONDER

GOD'S OWN TIME

READING ESTHER 4
'If you keep quiet at a time like this, God will deliver the Jews from some other source . . . who can say, but that God has brought you into the palace for just such a time as this?' (v. 14, LB).

When we are at our wit's end, only God can take over. Usually he takes over by using a person. Esther was the person chosen to save her people on this occasion. But notice, too, that the author says if Esther had been unwilling, then God would have raised up another to undertake the task of salvation. Sometimes it appears that salvation is never going to come. Many, indeed, throughout history have perished while waiting for salvation. Have they died because those who had been chosen to save them were unwilling to hear, or if they heard, were unwilling to act?

How many monks in the 14th and 15th centuries had come to the same conclusions as Luther, yet did not have the courage to make their views public in the way that he did? Did people perish because of that?

How many ship's captains were sickened by the slave trade in the eighteenth century? Even John Newton continued with that trade for some time after his conversion before speaking out against it. Surely people perished because of that.

How many people saw the deprivation in Victorian England before Bardardo, Shaftesbury and Booth, yet held back from speaking out? Did thousands perish because of that?

More recently, how many people saw the rotten-ness of the Shah's regime in Iran, yet failed to speak out? Surely thousands have since perished because of that. And so we could go on.

TO PONDER *Speaking out demands the courage Esther had, the courage to risk reputation, even life itself. Only then will God intervene to save, so dare we, even for a moment face the responsibility of **not** speaking out?*

TAKING THINGS PERSONALLY – I

READING ESTHER 5
' "Yes, and Esther the queen invited only me and the king himself to the banquet she prepared for us; and tomorrow we are invited again" ' (v. 12, LB).

Poor Haman! Esther's invitation to the banquet puts him almost on a level with the king. It is the fulfilment of his highest ambition. Without question everyone will now bow down to him, and nearly worship him. Persian kings were worshipped almost like gods. Haman saw himself very, very close to that position. Only one man stood in his way. Mordecai, the Jew.

Haman thought Mordecai's refusal to bow down was a personal insult. He thought Mordecai's claim that it was against Jewish principles to bow down, i.e. worship anyone but God, was merely an excuse. Haman could not see beyond his own self-importance. Equally, when Esther invited him to dine, he took that invitation personally. A less conceited man, or woman, would have assumed the invitation was due to the office they held, and not a personal one.

3:4

Because he took things so personally even his moment of triumph was spoilt. What should have been the happiest day of his life was ruined because one man refused to bow down to him. How petty! A moment's reflection and a few hours of study would have showed him the real reason for Mordecai's refusal. But conceited, proud people don't take the time or make the effort to look into the feelings and sensibilities of others.

Haman was to pay dearly for this mistake, but for the moment with his gigantic gallows built, ready to hang Mordecai, he goes on his way rejoicing!

TAKING THINGS PERSONALLY – II

READING ESTHER 6 & 7
'Haman thought to himself, "Whom would he want to honour more than me?" (6,6b, LB).

The security of a good position, indeed the best position in the government, and the honour of his private banquet with the King and Queen has clouded Haman's judgement. Faced with the question 'How should the king treat someone he wants to honour?' Haman immediately assumes he is the one! His sense of his own importance is boundless. His desire to be noticed and feted is overwhelming. He sets up a programme of celebration fit for the king himself.

Imagine his disappointment. Imagine the fear which struck him when he heard that Mordecai, whom he considered his greatest enemy, was the one the king chose to honour. What a sermon against excessive honour being paid to any one! The fawning to and flattery of 'great' men should be avoided at all costs. Learn from Haman's disaster.

Pay due respect to all, excessive respect to none.

The seriousness of Haman's position is not immediately obvious. No one knows Queen Esther is also Jewish. Perhaps Haman's wife has some idea, but we cannot tell how much even she knows. When Esther reveals her identity, Haman's shock at being told to honour Mordecai pales into insignificance. His fear now, is the fear of imminent death. Esther's reaction is understandable. Haman has threatened her family, friends and fellow Jews with destruction. To hang him on the gallows he prepared for another, it might be argued, is reasonable. But what follows is difficult to excuse on any grounds.

6:13

v. 10

REPEAT   *Pay due respect to all, excessive respect to none.*

SELF DEFENCE

READING ESTHER 8
'This decree gave the Jews everywhere permission to unite in defence of their lives and their families, to destroy all the forces opposed to them, and to take their property' (v.11, LB).

Throughout their history Jewish people have suffered much at the hands of their enemies. Time and again they are faced with the dilemma, how to react to persecution. Usually, but not always, the persecution is because of their religion. Religion is a matter of personal belief, of culture and morality. It is, particulary for Jews, a family matter. It is dependent also on the Scriptures, the Old Testament. So whenever Jews are persecuted because of their religion it is difficult for them to know how to react.

Any violent reaction, any tit-for-tat retaliation, goes against the very Scriptures for whose sake they are persecuted. Those Scriptures tell them. (Exod. 23:4; Prov. 24:29; Jonah 1:2 etc.)
To love their enemies.
That faithfulness to God involves suffering.
That taking the life of another is wrong.
That religion is an inward thing, a matter of the heart which cannot be removed by persecution. (Isa. 52:13–53:12)
Some specific laws, e.g. the law of Sabbath Observance, prevent them from working – and that includes defending themselves – on the Sabbath. (Exod. 20:13) (Jer. 31:33; Deut. 10:16; Mic. 6:6–8)

So when they do finally react, it is sometimes too late, as was the case in Germany before the war. It is sometimes too strong, as with Mordecai and Esther.

As I write, Israeli police have just gone on the offensive against rioting Arabs in Gaza and in Jerusalem. They have begun to act as though Esther's decree was still in operation. How far will that reaction go? As yet we cannot tell. Whatever happens, pray that those faced with the problems of a rejected people languishing in Gaza may begin to tackle the vast sea of misunderstanding, hate and power politics which has brought them to that place. Otherwise the history of Esther may repeat itself on a still greater scale.

A REASON TO CELEBRATE?

READING ESTHER 9 & 10
'The king issued a decree causing Haman's plot to boomerang' (9:25, LB).
'All the Jews throughout the realm . . . declared they would never cease to celebrate these two days at the appointed time each year' (9:27, LB).

We have already hinted it is hard to excuse wholesale slaughter of those who oppose the Jews. Is there any reason to celebrate? The declaration makes Haman's plot 'boomerang'. The Jews must do to Haman's men exactly what he'd planned to do to them and no more. Perhaps it means the king merely changed sides, so the Jews gained a military victory rather than staged a pogrom in reverse. Very different from a murderous 'police' operation. Also no plunder was taken (*10:16*). But even if Purim celebrates military victory rather than a slaughter of innocents, is it right?

The message of Esther hangs on that word 'boomerang', translated by *NIV* 'the evil scheme . . . should come back onto his own head' (*9:25*). The whole idea is of turning round. In the New Testament repentance means turning round. It is the same message that says 'The first shall be last and the last shall be first.' (*Matthew 19:30*) Esther holds out the promise that one day the tables will turn. So far in history such turning always seems to mean those who were oppressed become in turn the oppressors. But the cross of Jesus brings hope that the turning of the tables will lead, not to oppression, but to understanding and compassion, to real love of one's enemies instead of merely turning the tables on them. Then there will indeed be reason to celebrate.

PRAYER SUBJECT: *The displaced people of Gaza and the West Bank.*

PRAYER: *We pray for those who still suffer because of political decisions made two generations ago. We pray for a solution, Lord, despite the hopelessness of the situation. Although neither side acknowledges you, may both act sacrificially, not by using their supporters as sacrificial lambs, but by taking the sacrificial step of real negotiation in place of confrontation.*

READING COLOSSIANS 1:1,2
'From Paul, who by God's will is an apostle of Christ Jesus, and from our brother Timothy – To God's people in Colossae, who are our faithful brothers in union with Christ: May God our Father give you grace and peace' (vv. 1,2, GNB).

Greetings are a vital part of Paul's letters. They follow a pattern, very close to the formal pattern of all letters written in Paul's day.

1. The name of the writer, Paul the apostle.
2. The co-writer(s), where applicable. (Timothy was a good friend and helper in many different situations, not least as a sounding board for Paul's thought when the apostle was writing letters). *See 11 & 15 January*
3. The name of the recipient church. Here, the church at Colossae.
4. Often a word of explanation concerning his apostleship (not needed here).
5. The formal greeting. In Greek letters this was usually one word, Xairein. Paul changes this to a similar word, Xaris – Grace. Paul also invariably uses the Hebrew greeting 'peace'. *Gk. eirene, Heb. shalom*
6. Thanks for some aspect of the life of the church he is writing to (apart from Galatians). In Colossians, as usual, he thanks God for the faith of the church. He also brings a significant phrase into the earlier part of the greeting, calling them 'faithful brothers in **union** with Christ', because this letter is going to stress very strongly the idea of union with Christ. *v. 4*

Today's passage and comment is short, hoping that you will be able to read the whole of this letter at some point in the day. Treat it as though it had just come in the morning post. How exciting to receive a letter from Paul himself!

The Christian goal is not the outward and literal imitation of Jesus, but the living out of the Christ life implanted within by the Holy Spirit. UNION WITH CHRIST

(D. W. Lambert)

A CHURCH FOUNDER

READING COLOSSIANS 1:3–14
'You learnt of God's grace from Epaphras, our dear fellow-servant, who is Christ's faithful worker on our behalf. He has told us of the love that the Spirit has given you' (vv. 7,8, GNB).

vv. 7,8

4:12,13

Phil.
2:25–30,
4:18

Epaphras founded the Colossian church. Paul himself had never visited it, even though it was a busy place, not far from Ephesus. Had Epaphras been converted during Paul's two-year ministry there? We don't know. But everything we do know about Epaphras speaks of his faithfulness, his industry and his enthusiasm for the gospel.

These qualities are strikingly similar to those of his namesake Epaphroditus, Paul's messenger from Philippi. Scholars seem agreed that they were two different people, but knowing how mobile Paul was, and how he expected his fellow workers to move around with him or carry messages for him, there is a distinct possibility that Epaphras and Epaphroditus are one and the same. Their qualities of loyalty, steadfastness and industry are certainly very similar indeed.

Epaphras founded the church, but note how Paul emphasises that it is the Spirit who has implanted love in the hearts of Christians there. This is a mystery. We learn about God's grace from the preacher, and it is essential for every Christian to be involved in spreading the gospel. God uses preaching, teaching, – and even, I do believe, writing (!) – as a means of imparting his grace. All these and many other methods besides. Yet it is always the Spirit which implants love in the heart of the Christian. It is the Spirit alone who works – but mysteriously he works through us. We can and must teach people about the Lord we know. People need to see Christ reflected in our lives.

A THOUGHT *When God works, he does not by-pass us. He uses us to the limit of our capability and beyond what we think we are capable of!*

A SECOND EXODUS

READING COLOSSIANS 1:9–14
'He rescued us from the power of darkness and brought us safe into the kingdom of his dear Son, by whom we are set free, that is our sins are forgiven' (vv. 13,14, GNB).

Although Paul is writing for a church which lived and moved within a pagan society, he still uses some Old Testament pictures.

Paul describes the Christian life in today's verses as a deliverance like the deliverance of the people of Israel from Egypt. God rescues us from the power of darkness (Egypt), brings us safe into the kingdom (The Promised Land), and sets us free. It is a similar idea to one used in Paul's speech to King Agrippa, where he describes Jesus saying to him, 'I will rescue you . . . from the Gentiles to whom I will send you. You are to . . . turn them from the darkness to the light and from the power of Satan to God, so that through their faith in me they will have their sins forgiven.' *(Acts 26:17,18)*

Our personal deliverance from the sphere of darkness is as great as the deliverance of a whole nation from captivity. Not only that, Paul describes the deliverance as having already taken place. We are already fit to share 'in the kingdom of light.' The pity is, so few Christians take that idea really seriously. Paul dealt with a similar theme earlier. Our deliverance is a present reality. The transformation is not yet complete, but it has started. The life of holiness has begun. It is not instant perfection, but as Paul puts it so clearly '**We ask God to fill you with the knowledge of his will . . . Your lives will produce all kinds of good deeds and you will grow in your knowledge of God' (vv. 9,10).** *(1 Cor. 15, WoL 18 February)*

Help us to take seriously the fact that we are redeemed. Free us from burdening guilt so that, although we may be imperfect, we become aware of your indwelling, and of a growing likeness to yourself, Lord Jesus Christ. *(A PRAYER)*

THURSDAY 20 APRIL
THE PROPER PLACE

READING COLOSSIANS 1:15–20
'Christ existed before all things, and in union with him all things have their proper place. He is the head of his body, the church; he is the source of the body's life' (vv. 17,18, GNB).

Christ is the head. We are the body. No Christian can say 'I am the body of Christ.' Christians together can say 'We are the body of Christ.' If that is true, then it seems individual holiness, i.e. Christlikeness, is impossible. But Christlikeness is possible. Each of us can be indwelt by Christ, even though none can be THE body. This means we are indwelt by the very nature of God himself, by one v. 17 who 'existed before all things' and through whom 'God v. 16 created everything in heaven and earth, the seen and the unseen things'.

Today's verses are one of the highpoints of what is called Christology. The status given to Christ in these verses is higher than in the earlier letters of Paul. Here Christ is placed on the same level as God himself. Some scholars argue, vv. 15–20 are not from Paul himself but from an early Christian hymn, because their idea of Christ being equal to God is so extreme.

After 2,000 years it is easier to think of God and Christ as, in a sense, equal. We are used to the idea, expounded for centuries, that Christ is pre-eminent. But imagine how it seemed when Paul wrote. Christ's lifetime was closer than the fifties are to us. Think of Paul stating that someone so recently alive, remembered by many of his readers, 'existed before all things!' It is so astonishing, we cannot begin to understand, we can only v. 17 marvel and praise.

O for a trumpet voice,
On all the world to call,
To bid their hearts rejoice,
In him who died for all!
For all my Lord was crucified,
For all, for all my Saviour died.
(Charles Wesley)

PEACEMAKING

READING COLOSSIANS 1:20–23
'Through the Son, then, God decided to bring the whole universe back to himself. God made peace through his Son's death on the cross and so brought back to himself all things, both on earth and in heaven' (v. 20, GNB).

Peacemaking is a keynote phrase in Paul's thinking. Usually, as in most translations of Colossians 1:20 we use the more imposing word 'reconciliation' but *GNB* is a little more down to earth. Reconciliation is simply making peace. In human terms peacemaking requires give and take, negotiation, accommodating another person's point of view.

There are always changes on both sides if true peace is to be achieved.

Once again we cannot think in quite the same way where God is concerned. It is tempting to do so. Some are tempted to think that God changed when he sent Christ to atone for our sins. That would be false. God does not change. It is only our thoughts about him which change.

God makes peace with us by bringing us back to himself. He knows all the toils, troubles and turmoil which we go through. He has always known it. We recognise his knowledge of our pitiable condition by means of a historical event, the crucifixion which showed Jesus Christ, God's true image, suffering the ultimate agony of death with us, and on our behalf.

This view of peacemaking, reconciliation, atonement as a demonstration of God's identity with us is, admittedly, only part of the story. But it is an important part, which Charles Gabriel expresses poetically:

> *He took my sins and sorrows,*
> *He made them his very own;*
> *He bore my burden to Calvary,*
> *And suffered and died alone.*

SHARING IN CHRIST – I

READING COLOSSIANS 1:24–29
'And now I am happy about my sufferings for you, for by means of my physical sufferings I am helping to complete what still remains of Christ's sufferings on behalf of his body, the church' (v. 24, GNB).

Phil. 3:10–11

2 Cor. 4:10

Elsewhere, Paul talks of sharing the sufferings of Christ in order to know the power of his resurrection. He also claims that 'we carry in our mortal bodies the death of Jesus.' For him being 'in Christ' means going all the way, right to death itself. But it is only here in Colossians that this suffering appears to imply Christ's own suffering is in some way incomplete.

There are two ways to approach this. Firstly, we can understand that God in Christ still suffers with us. The sacrifice was completed on the cross. The sacrifice was perfectly sufficient to cover our sin, in every respect. But each sin that we commit in some sense also keeps on nailing him there. The same process which actually led him to the cross continues in today's world.

Mark 10:39

Secondly, and in a similar way, we each participate in that continuing suffering. When Jesus said 'You will indeed drink the cup I must drink and be baptized in the way I must be baptized' he really meant it. That word could not be fulfilled in his lifetime. It is fulfilled in every day and age, and goes on being fulfilled today.

FOR MEDITATION

We have commented on verse 24, the difficult verse in this passage. Read and re-read verses 25–29. Let them penetrate the very depths of your being and share that fellowship in Christ which has been the privilege of Christians throughout the ages. Christ is in you.

A THOUGHT

Christians feel the pain of Christ over a world which rejects him. Christians rejoice with Christ over each one who accepts him.

ARGUMENT – I

READING COLOSSIANS 2:1–10
'I tell you, then, do not let anyone deceive you with false arguments, no matter how good they seem to be' (v. 4, GNB).

Argument has always been a contentious matter for the Christian. On one hand some say God's Word is sufficient. Everything needed for salvation and maintenance of spiritual life is there. Keep to God's Word and argument will be unnecessary. We can never fully understand the infinite nature of God, so why not leave things to God alone, and maintain a simple faith!

That works for many, but if you have stayed with '*Words of Life*' as far as this, we may assume you don't quite hold that view. There is a curiosity, a need for the intellect also to be satisfied when dealing with the deep things of life. The danger is that, when argument is allowed full sway, it tends to take over. We become involved in speculation which may not be helpful, and may be dangerous.

But to maintain our faith against the arguments of the unrighteous, it must be a reasoned faith. Otherwise false arguments may divert us from the true faith before we know what has happened. At Colossae some people had obviously been teaching a dangerous heresy. It seems a pity Paul doesn't tell us what this false teaching was. We only know it existed, and from Paul's positive statements later in the letter, it may have had something to do with astrology; *(2:8; 'ruling spirits of the universe')* other pagan rites; *(2:16, the New Moon festival)* and possibly also with trying to make gentile Christians keep the Jewish law. *(2:11 'not with circumcision' 2:16 'or the Sabbath')*. Paul's advice is to keep Christ in the centre of our thinking, whatever arguments we employ.

TWO THOUGHTS: *1. Ignorance is more dangerous than argument.*

2. 'The devout minds of the church have always felt that their faith was compelled to seek to understand . . . They failed only when they thought they had understood without seeing yet more to be understood.' *(Ronald Wallace)*

PRAYER SUBJECT: *For wisdom.*

PRAYER: *Teach us, Lord, to know when and how to argue; and when to accept that argument can take us no further.*

SHARING IN CHRIST – II

READING COLOSSIANS 2:11–19
'For when you were baptized, you were buried with Christ, and in baptism you were also raised with Christ through your faith in the active power of God, who raised him from death' (v. 12, GNB).

On Saturday we emphasised the fact that Christians share in Christ's suffering. Today, while not forgetting that, we emphasise that Christians share in Christ's resurrection.

It is a new life that we share. The old life under law, afraid to put a foot wrong in case some trivial rule is being broken, is done away with. The new life is empowered by the resurrected Christ. Past sins and failings are covered, forgotten, done away with and we start anew. No longer do we have to survey our life as though it is a profit and loss account, trying to balance the good deeds against the bad, hoping the good will finally outweigh them, so that we come out on the profit side. Life in Christ is quite different. It involves starting afresh.

Paul uses the symbolism of baptism to illustrate this new start. First there is the death, the total immersion in the water, then the rising to life, rising from the water. The rite of baptism is a once-and-for-all experience. Sharing in Christ's death and resurrection life is a continuing experience. That continuing experience can be ours, if we seek the reality that baptism symbolises.

v. 13

v. 17

But what of those who knew no law previously? What of those who did just as they pleased and recognised no authority but their own desires? The same liberation applies. Christ frees those who are bound by self just as much as he frees those who are bound by the law. The reality is Christ, says Paul. That is the whole key to the new life.

FOR MEDITATION

Concentrating on Christ, allowing him full control, is the path to complete freedom.

READING COLOSSIANS 2:20–3:4
'You have died with Christ and are set free from the ruling spirits of the universe' (v. 20, GNB).

Christian doctrine has always been formulated against a background of heresy. Ideas are put forward by sincere, well-meaning Christian people trying to explain the gospel in terms which satisfy the mind. Then, instead of Christ being central, the explanation takes over the central place. That is the breeding ground for heresy.

Wol 23 April

Perhaps at Colossae someone had tried to explain the nature of Christ so that the Greek population would understand. Ancient Greeks believed the universe was made up of layers. Earth itself was the bottom layer and a succession of other spiritual layers led finally to the ideal, or the good. The in-between layers were the 'ruling spirits' which Paul mentions. It would be easy when explaining Christ to ancient Greeks to say he is a ruling spirit. But he then becomes one among many.

v. 20

It is a bit like trying to talk about Christ to a Hindu. Call Christ God and many Hindus will agree with you. They will say 'Yes, indeed, I believe that Christ is God.' They seem to be on the threshhold of commitment to Christ. But when you delve deeper you find they still see Christ as one amongst many Gods. Christ has simply been fitted in to a Hindu way of looking at the world.

We still have to try and explain. Jesus himself explained his role in simple terms. He called himself the Good Shepherd. The Son of Man, the One Who Is. None of these terms describes him fully. He is that, and much more. If we keep Christ central in our thinking we shall gradually come to understand. Our orientation will be towards heaven and earthly things will be placed in a proper perspective. Our life will indeed be 'hidden with Christ in God'.

John 10:11
John 6:53
John 6:20

Although God is in himself incomprehensible, unknowable, yet it is also His very nature to reveal Himself to his creatures.   *(D. M. Baillie)*

A PARADOX

A NEW SELF

READING COLOSSIANS 3:5–11
'You have taken off the old self with its habits and have put on the new self' (vv. 9,10, GNB).

22 January

This is one of Paul's clearest and most attractive pictures. We said 'Paul does not tell stories like Jesus did. The most we get is a vivid comparison of the Christian with some specific object, a little word picture perhaps, which illustrates some aspect of the Christian life.' Putting on a new self is one of Paul's best illustrations of the Christian's new life. It sounds like putting on or taking off a coat. He expands on this idea in vv. 12, 13, and also in Ephesians 6, 'Put on God's armour now!' where he describes the many different types of armour the Christian wears to fight and defend himself against the devil.

Eph. 6:13

The illustration has the great advantage of simplicity. It is also timeless, for however much technology changes it's unlikely we will cease to put on and take off clothes. It stresses the completeness of the change that putting on Christ involves. Putting on a new self means having a completely new outfit!

Its main drawback is that putting on and taking off is a daily occurrence. A new outfit doesn't in fact change us. The rich amongst us might even have a new outfit over and over again. But this new self in Christ – that is something else. It changes our whole attitude, not just superficially but right to the very depths of our being. It is so much more than a bath and a change of clothing. It reaches to our innermost feelings and desires.

I want that adorning divine,
Thou only, my God, canst bestow;
I want in those garments to shine
Which mark out thy household below.
(Charlotte Elliott)

A BRIDGE

READING COLOSSIANS 3:12–17
'So then, you must clothe yourselves with compassion, kindness, humility, gentleness, and patience. Be tolerant with one another and forgive one another whenever any of you has a complaint against someone else. You must forgive one another just as the Lord has forgiven you' (vv. 12,13, GNB).

Paul does not often quote Jesus directly. He shows familiarity with gospel teaching in a number of subtle ways. Today's passage contains a good example. 'Forgive one another just as the Lord has forgiven you.' It is a simple phrase which cleverly links two major points of Jesus' teaching. The words in the Lord's Prayer 'Forgive us the wrongs we have done, as we forgive the wrongs that others have done to us' and Jesus' words to the disciples 'Love one another as I have loved you.'

Matt. 6:12

John 13:34

Jesus: Love   as you have been   loved.
Paul: Forgive as you have been forgiven.

As we read on to verse 14 we see that the final article of clothing to be put on is love. That is the outer garment which binds all others together. Compassion, kindness, humility, gentleness and patience are all bound up with love. It reminds us of the great 'love' chapter. Even these lovely sounding qualities are nothing unless the outer garment of Christ-centred love to others binds all together. Christian love has its source in Christ. It comes from giving ourselves to Christ completely.

1 Cor. 13

> *The more I surrender to Jesus my Lord,*
> *The more of his fullness I know.*
> *The more that I give him the more he gives me,*
> *His grace and his peace he bestows.*
> *I cannot outgive him for he gave his all*
> *Can I do less than answer his call?*
> *The more I surrender to Jesus my Lord,*
> *The more of his fullness I know.*
> *(From 'Songs of the South' The Salvation Army, Atlanta,*
>   *Georgia)*

CULTURE SHOCK

READING COLOSSIANS 3:18–4:1
'Wives, submit to your husbands . . . Slaves, obey your human masters . . . Whatever you do, work at it with all your heart, as though you were working for the Lord and not for men . . . For Christ is the real Master you serve' (vv. 18,22,23, GNB).

v. 18

v. 22

Culture shock may hit us as we read Paul's practical advice on relationships. 'Wives, submit to your husbands' – and even more shocking 'Slaves obey your masters.' The second helps to put the first in context. I hope no one would argue that because Paul told slaves to obey their masters, abolition of slavery was wrong! Similarly, because Paul told wives to submit to husbands, no one should argue that sexual equality is wrong. Physical differences dictate different roles for men and women, e.g. men cannot bear children. That is the only absolute difference. Emotional differences exist, but none is absolute. More emotional difference exists between individual women, or between individual men, than between men and women as a whole.

Vigilance is needed to ensure that women are not deprived of rights because they are women; to ensure that equal opportunities are accorded to women and men; to ensure that women are not forced into certain roles simply because they are women, or men simply because they are men. We are continually being amazed at the 'men's' jobs that can be done by women – and the 'women's' jobs that can be done by men.

Equal vigilance is needed to ensure that women are not made to feel guilty because they accept and enjoy a traditional female role. Society forces women into roles they neither want nor enjoy at great risk to its own fabric.

LET PAUL
HAVE THE
LAST WORD

You were baptized into union with Christ, and now you are clothed, so to speak, with the life of Christ himself. So there is no difference between Jews and Gentiles, between slaves and free men, between men and women; you are all one in union with Christ Jesus.

(Galatians 3:27,28)

READING COLOSSIANS 4:2–5

'Be persistent in prayer, keep alert as you pray, giving thanks to God. At the same time pray also for us, so that God will give us a good opportunity to preach his message about the secret of Christ. For that is why I am now in prison' (vv. 2,3, GNB).

How strange, preaching a secret! But not so strange if we compare it with the practice of prayer. Christian prayer is an intensely personal matter. We pray as a congregation. We intercede out loud for each other. We praise God with loud voices. But our innermost thoughts and feelings are expressed most freely in times of personal prayer, the times when we are alone with our Lord.

Prayer is both a personal and a public matter, yet its operation is mysterious, secretive almost. We don't always want to wear our hearts on our sleeve and tell everyone about our most private moments talking to Jesus.

Similarly with proclaiming the gospel itself. It is a public matter. We need to shout it from the housetops to make the world hear. Yet it produces a deep, personal relationship between ourselves and God which is ours alone, which is mysterious, and which we cannot always communicate at the deepest level to other people. Always there is a sense of mystery, a feeling that there is still more to know and understand. The open secret of the gospel.

It's an open secret that Jesus is mine.   A POP SONG
It's an open secret this gladness divine.   FROM THE
It's an open secret, I want you to know,   SIXTIES
It's an open secret I love my Saviour so.
And you can seek him, find him, share the secret too,
Know his loving kindness in everything you do.
It's an open secret I want you to know,
It's an open secret I love my Saviour so.

(Joy Webb)

Share that secret today!

SHARING IN CHRIST – III

READING COLOSSIANS 4:6–18
'After you read this letter, make sure that it is read also in the church at Laodicea. At the same time you are to read the letter that the brothers in Laodicea will send you.' (v. 16, GNB).

Paul names lots of people in his final greeting, thirteen in fact. He is keen to establish good relationships with a Church he does not know personally, and encourage them to share with each other the good news of the gospel. In addition to the exchange of personal greetings, they are also to exchange letters.

The gems of instruction, words of advice, and doctrinal discussions found in the letter to Colossae are too good to keep to a small circle of friends. They need wider circulation. We can continue that circulation today, in a way Paul never dreamed of. He could give instructions to take the letter to Laodicea, a town close by Colossae. His successors, and we are all his successors, can take that same message to every corner of the globe.

As you read this you are sharing Paul's words along with thousands of others world-wide, from New Zealand to Sweden, from Africa to India, the USA and Canada, Singapore, the Philippines, Hong Kong, and many more. In great cities and isolated mission stations people will today complete a brief study of Paul's letter to Colossae. Pray for your fellow readers of the gospel, who gain inspiration through systematic study of God's Word just as you do. May that reading and study be translated into work and worship, as Paul intended when he asked Colossae to share with Laodicea.

Some readers may be known to you. Mention them by name. If you read in isolation, take comfort and strength from the fact that you are being remembered particularly in prayer today by other *Words of Life* readers.

PRAYER SUBJECT: *All students of God's word.*
BENEDICTION:
Paul's personal word to Archippus, which we can share
  'Be sure to finish the task you were given in the Lord's service.'
Paul's general word to us all
  'May God's grace be with you.'